3.1 PLAYS

BRUCE JAY FRIEDMAN

LEAPING LION
B O O K S

Leaping Lion Books logo designed by Kristina Konstantinova
Cover design by Dawn Brown
Author photograph by Molly K. Friedman

Library and Archives Canada Cataloguing in Publication

Friedman, Bruce Jay, 1930-
    3.1 plays / Bruce Jay Friedman.

Issued also in electronic format.
ISBN 978-0-9878241-0-3

    I. Title. II. Title: Three-point-one plays.

PS3556.R5T57 2012   812'.54   C2012-900507-X

Table of Contents

Preface

If Mark Twain were to be granted a day back on earth, would he recoil in horror when he saw that a new edition of Huckleberry Finn has turned "Nigger Jim" into "Slave Jim"? And what about Ernest Hemingway in the same situation? Would he want to have "black man" or "Afro-American" replace each of the many "nigger" references in his novel, "To Have and Have Not"?

I can't prove that they would object to these emendations, but my guess is that they would stand by the original. And what of the anti-Semitism in Evelyn Waugh and John O'Hara—and Shakespeare himself? (Though in the case of the Bard, some might reach for the argument that in the case of Merchant of Venice, there was no anti-Semitic intent.) Given the choice, would these classicists want to have their masterpieces "cleansed" and tailored to suit the times? And to have this process continue forever as labels and the culture continue to change? It seems unlikely.

These are highly presumptuous examples, but they represent a dilemma I faced when going over my plays, "Scuba Duba" and "Steambath," in particular. Both contain language that is considered offensive to women and blacks and Poles, and several other groups, no matter what the spirit in which they were spoken. Harold Wonder, the central character in Scuba Duba, is a particular "offender." Never mind that his wife has casually run off with a black man, that he suffers a two hour psychic castration on stage and that he lashes out with the only weapon available to him— i.e. the offensive racial epithets.

It would have been an easy matter to soften the language, to "update" it, to make the language palatable to a contemporary audience.

The plays were written and first performed half a century ago. There wasn't a single protest from the critics. Nor was there an outcry from any of the groups that might have felt offended. Indeed, both plays were warmly received. Both won awards: "Scuba Duba" in particular became the longest-running play in off-Broadway history. It ran for two years "without an empty seat," as I am always quick to point out, and would have continued on if I hadn't gotten bored with it. "Steambath" has had a great many productions both here and abroad. In Jerusalem, the role of the Puerto Rican towel attendant was played by an Israeli-Arab.

Some of the original language makes me wince. Yet I decided to let the original version remain and take whatever flak that comes as a result.

My wife, Patricia J. O'Donohue, is a teacher.

"If I were covering Kerouac," she said, "I'd want the raw files and not some bowdlerized and tarted up version of the text."

And of course she would put the play and the language in historical perspective.

And so here are the plays, "Warts and All", to quote the title of a book written by two of my sons, Josh and Drew Friedman. I am not the first to point out that when a book or play goes out to the world, it no longer belongs to the author. If a Baptist church in Philadelphia wishes to do a production and turn "fags" into "gays", "spades" into "Afro-Americans", they have my blessing. But don't count on me to show up for the opening. I'm a story-teller. I know the stories. And once I do, it's on to the next one. Much good luck and don't forget to send a cheque. The price of a candy bar has gone up considerably.

Bruce Jay Friedman

August, 2011

PUBLISHER'S NOTE

Bruce Jay Friedman was born on April 26, 1930. He grew up in the Bronx and studied journalism at the University of Missouri. While serving in the Air Force during the Korean War, he sent a short story he wrote to the distinguished magazine *The New Yorker* and, while the magazine turned that story down, it did publish his next attempt. Not long after, his stories began to appear in *Mademoiselle, Harper's, Esquire, Playboy, Tri-Quarterly, Saturday Evening Post*, and *Antioch Review*. His first novel, *Stern*, was published in 1962. This was followed by the novels *A Mother's Kisses* (1964), *The Dick* (1970), *About Harry Towns* (1974), *Tokyo Woes* (1985), *The Current Climate* (1989), *A Father's Kisses* (1996), and *Violencia!* (2002). His plays *Scuba Duba: A Tense Comedy* (1967) and *Steambath* (1970) were off-Broadway sensations, the latter being taped and presented as a television special on PBS. He has published six collections of stories, including *Three Balconies: Stories and a Novella* (2008), and a collection of nonfiction, *Even the Rhinos Were Nymphos* (2000). The movies *The Heartbreak Kid* (1972, 2007) and *The Lonely Guy* (1984) were adapted from stories of his, and he created, wrote, and/or contributed to the stories and screenplays for *Fore Play* (1975), *Stir Crazy* (1980), and *Splash* (1984). As an actor, he has appeared in the Woody Allen movies *Another Woman* (1988), *Husbands and Wives* (1992), and *Celebrity* (1998).

In addition to *Scuba Duba: A Tense Comedy* and *Steambath*, this volume includes *Sardines* and the very short play, *The Trial*. The first two, *Scuba Duba: A Tense Comedy* and *Steambath*, were produced off-Broadway at the *New Theatre* and the *Truck and Warehouse Company* in 1967 and 1971 respectively. Both were subsequently published in book form: we thank *Simon & Schuster* and *Alfred A. Knopf* for permission to reprint them here in substantially their original form. *Sardines* was produced on stage in East Hampton, New York in 1994 but has not been previously published. *The Trial* has not to this point been either produced or published.

In an appendix to the plays, we are reprinting several reviews that appeared contemporaneously with *Scuba Duba: A Tense Comedy* and *Steambath*. While these plays are enduring works of art, intelligence, and wit, they are also very much of their time. And in this case, this means that the language of the characters is modulated by conventions that may strike some as jarring today. Nevertheless, these two plays remain important not only as examples of some of the best work that was appearing off-Broadway in the 1960s and 1970s, but also as forerunners of the similarly "tense comedies" of David Mamet, Neil Simon, and John Guare of the 1970s and 1980s. It isn't hard to see why *Scuba Duba* was considered groundbreaking in 1967 (it ran for 692 performances), or why it continues to be considered a classic of the modern stage. This dark comedy, brimming with sexual and racial tension, cuts very close to the bone. To say that Harold Wonder, the white, Jewish protagonist of *Scuba Duba* who has "lost" his wife to a black scuba diver, is deeply distressed by the situation is an understatement: he is absolutely wild with humiliation and resentment. Harold is intimidated by what he believes to be the superior sexual prowess of his wife's black lover and has difficulty seeing through his anger to the truths that underlie his approach to his relationships. As the play makes clear, his wife has demeaned him sexually as a lover, so he's easy game for any rival. Like Lady Chatterley, she seems to respond sexually to someone of a lower social station, and is turned off by a husband whom she thinks of as intellectually superior to her. These corrosive ingredients set the stage for the "tense comedy" that unfolds as Harold confronts his wife and her lover.

In, the second play, *Steambath*, a young man named Tandy unexpectedly and unaccountably finds himself in a steambath. His last memory is of having been in his favorite restaurant, eating a double order of Won Shih pancakes. This is not an ordinary steambath, mind you. This one, as Tandy gradually realizes, is run by God (a Puerto Rican who doubles as the bath attendant) and is evidently a station on the way to whatever it is that follows life. All Tandy's fellow bathers have died, and so, to Tandy's great distress, has he himself. Tandy just can't accept this situation: "The timing is all wrong," he says. He's in the middle of writing a novel, he's gotten over his divorce, and has a great new girlfriend and a good relationship with his ten-year-old daughter. He decides to approach God to "get this straightened out." "You addressing I?" God says. The ensuing confrontation provides a lucid, surprising, and hilarious colloquy about the absurdity of life and death.

The third play, *Sardines*, is a highly comical love story set in the late sixteenth century. It begins with an announcer's prologue: "This is the story of the Spanish Armada, the man who led it, the strange circumstances under which he was chosen to command, and his adventures, both romantic and otherwise, as they might have happened. It has been suggested that the fate of the Armada holds a lesson for us in our own troubled times. The author doubts this, but is willing to be convinced." Sardines does not trade in the dark racial satire of the previous two plays; its rather more rollicking comedy is exemplified by the following exchange by Don Pedro Ferrara and Dona Antonia Navarre after one of the battles:

> *Antonia: Don Pedro, what on earth is going on?*
> *Don Pedro: We've captured the Santa Ana.*
> *Antonia: But that's wonderful news.*
> *Don Pedro: Not really. It's one of our own ships.*

The final play, a one-act lagniappe called *The Trial*, involves a theft, a humiliation, a visit, and a reversal. The theme of the play is the consequence of one's acts, even trivial acts, over the long span of one's life. The surprise is only half the story.

These four plays constitute a small portion of Bruce Jay Friedman's prodigious literary output but are not unrepresentative in the incisive humor he brings to his work. What you have in your hands is, as Richard Watts, Jr., said of *Scuba Duba* in the *New York Post*, "a wild and cheerful exhibition of meaningful lunacy."

3.1 PLAYS

BRUCE JAY FRIEDMAN

SCUBA DUBA

A TENSE COMEDY

4 Bruce Jay Friedman

Character List

HAROLD WONDER — Young man (thirty-five or thereabout), wearing a bathrobe, pajamas, and slippers.

MISS JANUS — Harold's young neighbour, quite pretty, and wearing a bikini.

DR. SCHOENFELD — An acquaintance of Harold's, whom Harold believes offers good advice.

TOURIST — An American, middle-aged robust man.

LANDLADY — French woman, slightly past middle-age.

MOTHER — Harold's mom, prone to laying on guilt trips.

CHEYENNE — A wild-looking blonde.

JEAN WONDER — A young (early thirties), attractive lady, rather forlorn at the moment and prone to bumping into things. She is gentle in manner.

FROGMAN — A Negro in full undersea regalia, spear gun in hand, and flippers on feet.

REDDINGTON — A pipe-smoking intellectual Negro man, quite good-looking in aesthetic way.

ADDITIONAL CAST — Thief, Gendarme.

ACT I

SCENE   (*Main room of château. South of France. Early evening.*
                 HAROLD WONDER, *visibly upset, paces back and forth,
                 holding a large gardener's scythe, but seems unaware it
                 exists. Someone is playing a piano in a neighbouring house,
                 something loud, abrasive, in the style of Khachaturian's
                 "Sabre Dance." He goes to the window, looks toward the
                 source of the music.*)

HAROLD WONDER   (*With irony.*)

                 I really needed this. This is exactly what I came here for.

                 (HE *opens the window and gestures with the scythe, calling
                 out at the same time.*)

                 Hello! Hey!

                 (*Music stops* MISS JANUS *appears.*)

MISS JANUS   Hi.

HAROLD   Hey. Thanks for dropping in. I'm not allowed to leave,
                 myself.

                 (*Defensively.*)

                 I don't need anyone's permission. It's just better if I stay
                 here.

MISS JANUS

I thought you might have a giant bird flying loose around here and called me over to help. Every few months someone does that to me. I seem to give the impression I'd know what to do about people's loose birds.

HAROLD

(*Distantly.*)

I wish that's all it was. I wish I could turn the whole thing into a bird problem.

(*Coming back.*)

I thought you'd look different. I thought you'd be a little, I don't know, a little noisier looking.

(HE *has been using the scythe to accompany his speech.*)

Oh this? I'm sorry. I just picked it up and started carrying it around. Well, I didn't just pick it up. Actually, we had a prowler a few nights ago. My wife opened the shutters and came face to face with him, some kind of Swede she said it was. With a frying pan on his head.

MISS JANUS

(*Making herself at home.*)

Maybe he just wanted to go through your wife's purse. Not to steal anything, but just to see what was in it. I had a Syrian friend once who loved to do that. We had a thing where I'd fill up my purse, pretend to be asleep, and then he'd tiptoe in and go through it. I put all kinds of surprises in there for him – birth control pills, religious ornaments, surgical appliances, pictures of other Syrian guys...

HAROLD

I don't think he was after any of that. I think he was after much bigger stuff. Look, I'm here with my wife.

Except for the slight problem that I'm suddenly not here with my wife. That she decided not to be here.

(*Gesturing with scythe.*)

On that prowler I mentioned, it doesn't show, but I'm actually big enough under these things to take care of any trouble by myself.

(*Referring to scythe.*)

It's just something I do. Whenever there's trouble I pick up things. A friend of mine and I once started a little fight, just for fun. Before we began, I remember unconsciously picking up a chicken. One of those ready-made roasted things. I wasn't going to use it or anything. You can imagine how much good it would do you in a fight. Fly all over the goddamned place. I just seem to need something in my hands.

MISS JANUS   You're probably a very tactile person. I am, too.

(SHE *gets up and flicks at her bikini bottom.*)

Listen, does this fit or doesn't it? I bought it today and there were some German girls who said it was too small and I was hanging out of it. They could only speak about four words of English, but they managed to get that much across.

(*In imitation of German accent.*)

"Madame…from the bottom…you are too wide…"

(*Resuming normal style.*)

They'd been trying on bikinis and *theirs* didn't fit, so it may be they were just trying to spoil mine. The proprietor said it was because they were from

Düsseldorf. Düsseldorf girls try them on all day long and never buy them. That must be some city – Düsseldorf.

HAROLD

Look, I don't want to know Düsseldorf. I'm in the middle of something awful. Something that's really ripping me up. That happened tonight. But I just want you to know that your suit fits. Right out of my terribleness I know it fits. I never saw anything fit like that in my entire life.

MISS JANUS

I wish I could get to the state where I truly believe my ass was beautiful.

HAROLD

It'll happen. Just give it time.

MISS JANUS

Want me to tell you something I've never told anyone in my whole life? I was working in a place in the Village when I first came to New York. They had an ad that said they only wanted girls who looked like Modigliani paintings. Well, I was *feeling* kind of Modigliani-ish, so I went over and I got the job. It was a little disappointing. I was expecting hippies, acid heads, flower-power… It turned out to be a hangout for electricians. Well, there were five guys with long hair who at least *looked* a little Villagey and I'd pretend they were exotic types even though they kept talking about—what are those electric things?

HAROLD

Volts? Amperes?

MISS JANUS

That's the one, amperes. For a couple of weeks they never really said anything to me except "Another cappuccino." And then one morning—can you imagine, it was broad daylight—they said they'd like to take some pictures of me. Even then I knew what kind of pictures they meant. When I was off at eleven, I said, very business-like, "Okay, I'll go with you and take a few..."

(*Trails off as though the story is over.*)

HAROLD (*Completely hooked.*)

So?

MISS JANUS Oh! So I followed them to a brownstone and we started off with some madonna-like portraits and then, because I really knew what it was all about, I took off all my clothes without them even asking. And that was just for openers. They started moving the camera around and I started moving myself around and I was carrying on as though I were in a trance. I don't know how long it took, but then I heard a ship's horn in harbour and I put on my clothes and went home.

HAROLD Did you...?

MISS JANUS ...Sleep with them? No. I'm not sure really whether I wanted to or whether I would have. But I didn't.

HAROLD That's some story. I loved it and everything, but that's some story. You just walked in here and sat down and I'm your neighbour and that's the kind of story you tell? I did love it, though. I hated it and I loved it.

MISS JANUS I know. I did too. I hated it and I loved it and I knew you would too. I could tell.

HAROLD Look, I'm in bad trouble. You remember that wife I mentioned earlier? She pulled something real cute on me. If I wasn't so embarrassed I'd be shaking like a leaf. I've got two kids sleeping upstairs. Until you came over I'd just been calling up people. I tried to get Dr. Schoenfeld in Monaco. Thank God I thought of him.

MISS JANUS   Don't tell me. He's your analyst.

HAROLD   Uh-uh. I don't fool around with that stuff. He's just a guy I know who lives in my building and happens to be a psychiatrist. I talk to him a lot in elevators and I seem to just bump into him in clothing stores, places like that. It's the most extraordinary thing. All he has to do is say three words to me and I feel better.

                 (*Cut-out of* DR. SCHOENFELD *appears.*)

                 I was fired from a job once. It was a big argument over whether I was allowed to use the executive john. Later I started to make more money than ever—but the idea of being fired was destroying me. So Dr. Schoenfeld says...

SCHOENFELD'S
VOICE   You're good at looking up and down, Harold, but you've never once looked at life sideways...

HAROLD   ...I never once looked at life sideways. He was suggesting I start looking at my problems out of the corner of my eye. It doesn't sound like much, but I tried it...

                 (*Demonstrating.*)

                 You know, there's a hell of a lot going on over there on the sides.

                 (DR. SCHOENFELD'S *cut-out disappears.*)

                 I have to call him in a little while. Look, I feel much better now, even though that electrician story of yours got me a little nervous. I feel like a damned fool about why I called you over in the first place.

MISS JANUS	You probably wanted to borrow something.
HAROLD	Well, actually, it was the piano. It was getting me jumpy. But now that I've met you, I'm sure it wouldn't bother me. You can play all you like.
MISS JANUS	It's nice when you look at my eyes. I just realized that hardly anyone ever does that. People look at my lips, my neck, my feet...
HAROLD	I took a quick peek at your feet, but I guess I mainly looked at your eyes. The trouble was I didn't know who was playing. It might have been anyone. But now that I know you're friendly, you can bang away to your heart's content.
MISS JANUS	Say, what do you do?
HAROLD	I'm in billboards. I write the stuff on them.
MISS JANUS	I'll bet you're great at it.
HAROLD	About three years ago some Bennington girl wrote an essay for the *Partisan Review* that said the prose on my billboards was the true urban folk literature of the sixties, much more important than Faulkner...

(*Considers this, clucks his head as though to say "Can you imagine anything that far-fetched?".*)

Look, I'm expecting these phone calls. But really, you can do anything you like. You can burn incense if you like and blow it into my chimney. I mean you've gotten me through a little piece of the night and that's the whole deal. If I can just make it through to the morning I'll be able to handle things a little better.

(HAROLD WONDER'S LANDLADY, *enters with a prospective* CLIENT *for the house—presumably for the month after the* WONDERS *vacate.*)

TOURIST

Well, I like it. It's French. And you can tell it's French. It smells French. I mean, the goddamned air is French. As long as you're going to be in the country I think you ought to just jump in and French it up. Like these salesgirls. Cute little biscuits, but did you ever get a whiff of them? Now ordinarily I'd haul off and tell them what I think of them but, what the hell, you're in France. I just let them go ahead and stink up the place. It's their country.

LANDLADY

Excuse me, I was just showing the château for when you leave.

(*To* MISS JANUS.)

You are in the films, no?

MISS JANUS

No.

(*Leaving.*)

LANDLADY

You're not in the films?

MISS JANUS

No.

LANDLADY

(*To* TOURIST.)

She's in the films.

MISS JANUS

Bye.

(SHE *leaves.*)

LANDLADY

Au revoir, mademoiselle... I know that face...

(*To* TOURIST.)

Françoise Sagan has had this house. Charles Aznavour. Brigitte Bardot was down for the summer with Jacques Tati. We have had Irving de Gaulle.

TOURIST   Irving de Gaulle?

LANDLADY   He is a brother of Charles, but he stays very quiet. They say he tells Charles exactly what to do, but in a whisper so no one will know. I myself have heard him pick up the phone in this very house and tell his brother to, how you say, screw Algeria.

(*Turning to* HAROLD.)

Excuse me, monsieur, we are through in five seconds.

(*To the* TOURIST.)

Monsieur Wonder is here because at the last second your Steve McQueen called to say he could not make it.

HAROLD   It's a little late.

TOURIST   Now that's the kind of talk I like. It's late and you just came right out and said it was late. It's not *that* late, actually, but that's not what I'm getting at. I think you ought to call a thing what it is. I got this guy, works for me and he's bald, see. Oh, he's got a little swirl of a thing sitting back there on his head and he kind of brings it forward, but for Christ's sake, the man is a skinhead, no two ways about it. Well, I could putter around and pretend I don't even notice it, you know, kind of kid him along. But I don't, see. He comes into my office every morning with a report and I don't let two minutes go by before I say "Hey there, Small" – that's his name – "I see you're parting your hair in the middle." Now he chokes up a little and I'm not about to say that he eats it up exactly – but for Christ's sake, I've laid the thing right out on the table instead of pretending it's not there. And, of course, to spare his feelings I've kind of blended it in with a little humour, which I believe in doing. The parting your hair in the middle part. That's humourous. It's not like I said "Get your tail in here, you bald son of a bitch" or anything. They do that in some offices. But I kind of skirt around the edges. That's how I keep my employees. You got a Chink's around here?

LANDLADY   Monsieur?

TOURIST   A Chinese restaurant.

HAROLD   There's a Vietnamese place around five miles down the road.

TOURIST   As long as they got those eggrolls I don't care what kind of Chink they are. I been all over the world, but I can't really settle into a place unless I know there's a good Chink's nearby. I understand they're opening them up all over Moscow. We got one in my town, a kind of drive-in Chink's. Night he opened up I was first in line. I said to him "You're pretty goddamned lucky to be here, buster." He looked kind of puzzled, but he knew damned well what I was talking about. I said to him "Let's say the dice had taken an extra roll. You could have been over there in Shanghai someplace starving to death." They got four-year-old prostitutes over there, I understand. Girl gets to be eight and she's still got her cherry, old Mao Tse-tung gives her a goddamned peace prize. You know what I'm talking about. "You'd have had beri-beri by now if you'd been over there. So you just keep those eggrolls *hot*, Mr. Chinkhead, and everything'll be all right." ... We never had any trouble with the guy. Hell, for all I know he could have been a *citizen* or something, but that gets us right to my philosophy. Lay it on the line.

HAROLD   (*To* LANDLADY, *temper snapping.*)

Look, in case anyone forgot, this is my house until September first. I'm not interested in any Elks' Convention. Would you mind just clearing out of here? I've got some calls coming and I'd like a little privacy.

TOURIST   That's all right, son, that's frank talk. We're not really intruding, the way I see it, but you think we are and you said so. No need to apologize. I like it here. I think I'll take it. It's French. Got a little of that salesgirl smell to it.

(*Leaving.*)

Take it easy, son, and don't take any wooden frogs' legs.

(TOURIST *exits.*)

LANDLADY   Ah, wonderful. I call Charlton Heston immediately and tell him sorry the house is rented.

(*Writing in a little book.*)

Alors, that takes care of September. He is charming, non? I think he is a famous actor.

HAROLD   For Christ's sake, he's *not* a famous actor.

LANDLADY   No, no, I am never wrong about these things. I think he is Tony Curtis. Yes, I'm sure of it. Tony would not want to make a big fuss over it, you know how they are. I notice madame is not here.

(*Primping.*)

HAROLD   You notice goddamned right.

LANDLADY	(*Seductively, humming a little romantic refrain.*)
	When I was a little girl I was the fairest flower in all Provence. They would come from miles around to gaze at me. And when there was a man I admired, my petals would open, one by one – floop, floop, floop.
HAROLD	Look, that's the last thing I want to hear about right now.
LANDLADY	And I have a secret for you, monsieur. My petals still open, not as often perhaps, but wider than ever.
HAROLD	Look, madame, I'm sure you were a winner in the old days and that you're still standing room only. But don't you see I'm a wreck?… Anyway, how come you didn't do anything when I shouted last night?
LANDLADY	You mean when we had the prowler?
HAROLD	When *I* had the prowler. I had to look in the guidebook to find out how to yell for help. Didn't you hear me? *Au secours, au secours!* I felt like a goddamned jackass.
LANDLADY	(*Correcting pronunciation.*)
	Se-cours. Ours. *Say! Se-Cours!*
HAROLD	(*Trying it.*)
	Secours.
LANDLADY	That is much better. What about the police, monsieur?
HAROLD	Oh sure, I know about the police. I got a cop on the phone and explained what happened. He said the only way he'd come is if I drove over there and watched the station for him. They've got one cop for the whole goddamned South of France. Look, madame,

I appreciate your company. I really do. But I'm in terrible trouble and I'm expecting these phone calls. I can't really talk when anyone's around. When I was a teenager I'd have to take all my calls in the closet. I'd put all these overcoats over my head. It's the only way I feel private.

LANDLADY   All right, monsieur, I understand. But remember that madame has a special cure for young men. The wonders of France. Your Jimmy Cagney was in such trouble. He comes to madame and poof, he wins the Oscar.

(SHE *leaves.* HE *smokes, putters around nervously, looks at phone, decides against it. Goes to window with scythe. Opens shutters, hollers out* au secours, au secours—*first loudly, then breaking off into a plaintive cry. Phone rings.* HE *picks it up, still holding scythe.*)

HAROLD   New York? Yes, operator, I'll take it.

(*Cut-out of* MOTHER *appears.*)

Hello, Mom.

MOTHER'S VOICE   Is that you, Harold?

HAROLD   Yeah, Mom, all the way from France.

MOTHER'S VOICE   What happened, sweetheart?

HAROLD   Nothing, Mom, nothing at all. I just decided to call. But I'll have to make it fast because it's costing a goddamned fortune. I don't even know how much. Oh Christ, I can't concentrate. It's too expensive.

MOTHER'S VOICE   First tell me about the children, sweetheart.

HAROLD   They're fine.

MOTHER'S VOICE	And is it nice in France?
HAROLD	It's wonderful, Mom. A wonderful country.
MOTHER'S VOICE	Harold, you have something heavy in your hand, don't you?
HAROLD	(*Looking at scythe, then dropping it.*)
	How the hell did you know that?
MOTHER'S VOICE	I've been your mother for a long time, darling.
HAROLD	Jesus, it must have cost a grand already and I haven't even said anything. Look, Ma, I'm in lousy trouble, so I'm just calling up people. I just want it to hurry up and be tomorrow morning.
MOTHER'S VOICE	Something did happen to the children. I knew it.
HAROLD	No, Mom. I told you they're fine.
MOTHER'S VOICE	Is your wife at your side—where she belongs?
HAROLD	No, Mom, Jean is out. That's what it's all about.
MOTHER'S VOICE	I knew it. I could have predicted the whole thing. Who is she out with, darling?
HAROLD	Mom, I can hardly get it out of my mouth. She's run off with a frogman.
MOTHER'S VOICE	A frogman, darling?
HAROLD	She's run off with a goddamned black scuba diver!
MOTHER'S VOICE	Don't talk that way, Harold. It's not nice.
HAROLD	All right, Mom. She's with a dark-skinned phantom of the ocean depths. Is that better? How do you think I

feel saying something like that on the phone and you don't think I said it politely enough?

MOTHER'S VOICE   (*Still calm, although news is sinking in now.*)

A frogman. That's what she needed, a frogman. You know why she's doing that, don't you, Harold? Because you didn't do enough for her. None of us did. The whole family didn't strip itself naked enough for her. And what did you give her, Harold? The French Riviera? That isn't a vacation, darling, that's a punishment. Didn't you know that? That's where you take people instead of throwing them into dungeons. You know where I would have taken her, Harold? I would have brought her back to that ghetto in Baltimore where you found her on the streets!

HAROLD   (*Interrupting.*)

Look, now don't go too far. You're not exactly a bargain yourself, you know!

MOTHER'S VOICE   Harold, I think there's something wrong with the connection. You couldn't possibly have said what I just heard you say.

HAROLD   How about that cello player you took me up to see when I was seven years old? You forgot him, eh? And that guy who made those alligator handbags. Never heard of him, eh? Well, I didn't forget them so easy. It didn't exactly do me any good to be in on that stuff, so don't go picking on Jean.

MOTHER'S VOICE   Is that why you called, Harold? You thought your mother needed a little filth thrown in her face. All the way from France.

HAROLD   All right, Mom, I'm sorry. I didn't mean to get into that.

MOTHER'S VOICE   (*In tears.*)

That's all right, Harold. I'll just consider that my payment after thirty-six years of being your mother.

HAROLD   I think she's going to stay out the whole night and I'm not sure I can take it. I'm waiting for a call now. I'm all alone here.

MOTHER'S VOICE   Harold, you know what your mother's going to do now? She's going to quietly take a plane and she's coming right over to France.

HAROLD   All right, all right. I'm calm now. Look, I have to say goodbye. This call is costing around twelve grand already.

MOTHER'S VOICE   And you promise me you'll use your head?

HAROLD   I promise. But if you hear the phone again from France, don't get nervous.

MOTHER'S VOICE   Believe me, sweetheart, you forget, but I've been through much worse than this. A mother doesn't forget. Much worse, Harold. This is a little nothing.

HAROLD   I know, Mom. There's just something about her staying out all night in a foreign country. Listen, are you sure you're okay?

MOTHER'S VOICE   Wonderful, Harold. I saw this *Virginia Woolf* they're all raving about. Frankly, I wouldn't give you two cents for Elizabeth Taylor!

HAROLD   I got to go now, Mom.

MOTHER'S VOICE   Goodbye, darling.

(THEY *exchange half a dozen goodbyes; finally* HAROLD *hangs up, cutting her off in the middle of one, and* MOTHER *cut-out disappears.*)

HAROLD

That was a fast eighty-seven dollars for a goodbye. I don't care. I'll talk to myself. What do I care? There's no law. As long as it makes me feel better, that's the only thing.

(*Goes to window. Shouting.*)

Jeannie, you bitch. France you picked to pull this on me. Not in Queens where I have defences. Where I have friends.

(*Plaintively.*)

Au secours, au secours.

(*Hears piano playing, sweet, melodic.*)

That's okay. That's fine. It doesn't bother me anymore. Now that I know she's friendly... It's one of my favourite mazurkas.

(*Goes to the window and yells out.*)

You can play it all night if you like.

(*Music stops.*)

(MISS JANUS *appears, still in bikini, eating from a fruit bowl.*)

MISS JANUS

Hi, could you hear me playing? I came over to find out.

HAROLD

No. I mean, I could, but it was fine.

MISS JANUS

Want some fruit? Make you strong.

HAROLD

I couldn't get anything down.

MISS JANUS	(*Eating away.*)
	It's like eating pure strength. I'm not fooling.
HAROLD	I never saw anyone eat fruit like that. You're kind of slopping it up and licking your fingers, and what is it? It's wonderful.
	(*Switching.*)
	Look, I'm in all this trouble. You probably guessed it's about my wife. And this coloured scuba diver.
	(*Chanting louder and louder.*)
	Scuba duba duba. Scuba duba duba. Scuba duba duba. That's what keeps bounding through my head.
	(*Cut-out of giant ape-man appears for a moment. Jungle drums are heard. Cut-out disappears.*)
MISS JANUS	You really are upset. Would you like me to cradle your head?
HAROLD	What do you mean?
MISS JANUS	(*Making a cradling gesture at her bosom.*)
	In here. Sometimes that's all people need, people with the world's toughest exteriors.
HAROLD	(*Trying it but unable really to fit into a good cradle.*)
	I don't think I'm doing it right. Anyway, it's hard to just sail into one of those.
MISS JANUS	All right, but if at any time you feel the need…just signal me.
	(SHE *demonstrates with cradling pantomime.*)

And we'll start right in, no formalities…

HAROLD   Okay, but meanwhile, if I start acting funny, just shove a little applesauce into me. It's in the kitchen. If you can just be with me awhile.

MISS JANUS   I can stay as long as you like. I was just château-sitting for my friend Abby and her new husband. Abby and I were roommates in New York while she was going with him. He's a sculptor named Nero. For three years she couldn't even get him to *talk* about marriage – until two months ago when she had her left breast removed. Suddenly Nero felt responsible as hell, wanted to marry her immediately. She hadn't come out of the ether and he had her in front of a minister. Abby wouldn't let me move out – it was almost as though she felt sorry for me for having both my breasts and having to be single. So I kind of tagged along with them to France. Something's supposed to happen between the three of us. I'm not sure what. It hasn't yet, but it's always in the air. At least once a day someone says "What'll we do tonight?" Then the air gets very tense. I think it would have happened already, but no one knows how to start. Or who's supposed to do what to who. And then there's always Abby's breast to worry about. How are you supposed to work that in?

HAROLD   (*Abashed.*)

You walked in here with some collection of stories…

MISS JANUS   Maybe some night Nero will say "Let's go, girls" and we'll all take off our clothes. Simple as that.

HAROLD   (*Looking out shutters.*)

You know, my wife's got the goddamned car. What am I supposed to do, take a taxi to Marseille, get out and say, "Pardon me, did you see this American woman and this black person with flippers on his feet?" He wears them out of the water, right on the goddamned sidewalk! He's graceful in them too, that's the awful part. Got one of those Jean Paul Belmondo styles. I mean what am I supposed to do, say he looks like W. C. Fields just because he's out jazzing my wife and I'm here with two kids trying to get through the goddamned night? I'm sorry. Please go on.

MISS JANUS

I think what's supposed to happen is that Abby is going to die and then Nero and I are logically supposed to more or less blend together. Say a month or so later. None of us have ever said it, but you guess that's what it's all about. We're waiting for Abby to die. He's very attractive and everything, but I wish he'd really wait. Like yesterday, Abby was out at the beach somewhere gathering shells—she gets beautiful ones now, the most exquisite you've ever seen, almost as though they've been left for her because she's going to die. He came up behind me, put his hands very deliberately on my two breasts almost as though he was counting them, and asked me to inhale something he keeps in a sponge. Well, all it does is make my ass itch a little. I've taken them all—pot, mescaline, LSD—I get a little sleepy and then my ass itches.

HAROLD

Look, there's something you ought to know.

MISS JANUS

Yes?

HAROLD

I'm a married man.

(*Chuckling ironically.*)

Some married. You know, she's had a series of these guys, not really *had* them as far as I know, but all they have to be is slightly worthless and she gets turned right on.

(*Cut-outs* of THREE MEN *appear in the room   one with floor-waxing equipment, a second in trunks with a swimming pool vacuum, and a third with a garbage man's trash sticker.*)

The first one was a floor shellacker. Then there was this guy who cleaned up swimming pools in Barbados. So help me, Christ, there was a garbage collector in Baltimore. He was a little classier than the rest of the garbage crowd. He'd only handle metal and wood. Left the mushy stuff to the other boys, but he was a garbage man all right, no matter how you slice it. It's a classical kind of deal. She can only relax with a man when she feels he isn't worth four cents. If he knows the alphabet, he's finished.

(*Cut-outs of* THREE MEN *disappear, arms locked in camaraderie.*)

I once tried acting a little low-down myself. I started hanging around the house in these Puerto Rican clothes. So one day Jeannie reached into my jacket and grabbed this extra inch of fat I have around my waist and wouldn't let go – she was letting me know who I was, underneath all the clothes. She wouldn't let go until I hit her. Came down hard on one of her pressure points. There's one in there, right around the shoulder blades. I used to memorize lists of pressure points and erogenous zones...

(*Switching.*)

Listen, why the hell don't you just move away from your friends?

MISS JANUS

I've drifted in with them and I don't seem to be able to drift out. It's that drifting I can't get over. It was that way the first time too. Men like to hear about the first time. I was going with a boy and my father didn't really like him so one night he pointed a gun at the boy's head and went "Pow." Like a joke. Only I got very nauseous and the next thing I knew the boy and I were drifting out to the highway and we sort of drifted into this shed that was full of old magazines and newspapers from all over the world. I let him make love to me right in the middle of all those publications. I can still remember their names.

(*Closing her eyes, and in a sort of religious chant, enunciating each one very deliberately.*)

The Philadelphia *Bulletin*, the Des Moines *Register*, the *Deutschlander* Verlag, *Paris-Soir*, the Sacramento *Bee*, the Newark *Star-Ledger*, Variety, the *Bulletin of Atomic Scientists*...

HAROLD

You know, I really love the kind of stories you tell, the kind where those things happen to you. Look, I don't know what comes next, you're terribly attractive, the way you eat fruit, for example, but I'm in the middle of this thing.

(*Hollering out window.*)

Come on out and fight, you black son of a bitch. Jeannie, I dare you to produce him now that I know what his game is!

(*To* MISS JANUS.)

I don't even know my own name. I've got these kids asleep upstairs. But couldn't we have this thing together in which you just tell me those stories—even if nothing else happens? They kind of sneak up on me—like a hug or something.

MISS JANUS   They never worked on Juan.

HAROLD   All right, let me sit down for this one. I'm sitting down for Juan.

MISS JANUS   He was just an eight-year-old boy in a slum school where I worked as a substitute teacher. Everyone in the whole school had tried to get through to him—but he kept on being sullen and withdrawn, wouldn't say a word, wouldn't meet your eyes. So then I took a crack at him. I told him all these stories. And at the end he was just as sullen and withdrawn as before.

HAROLD   That's the whole Juan story? That's what I sat down for? Look, I'll tell you quite frankly—I didn't like the material in that one. But I liked every one up to now. I love them even though they wreck me. I mean did you see me at the window with that black son of a bitch routine? Well, it's true. I really would like to run this…

(*Gesturing with scythe.*)

… right through his gizzard. But look, let's face it, you know the type of fellow I am—the straightest guy in France, right? Well, the truth is, I encouraged the whole thing. Just the way I'm getting you to tell those stories. What happened is that we met the bastard in Cannes one afternoon, right after we got here, standing around at one of those sidewalk restaurants with his flippers on and this black suit and that breathing equipment on his back. Wait a minute.

(*Goes to slide machine.*)

You want to hear something? I even took pictures of the goddamn thing.

(*As he is pulling a very long screen out of a very small closet.*)

Take a seat. Any seat in the house.

(MISS JANUS *complies. First slide of* FROGMAN *comes into focus.*)

There he is… Now, you take away the skin-diving stuff and he isn't really that handsome, but he has this smile that shows up now and then. It's as though he has a zipper across his mouth. He kind of unzips that smile and when you see his teeth it kind of puts him in a different league… Anyway, all summer long we'd been hearing about this wonderful loup fish, and Jeannie, who's one of the original fish-eaters, was really starved for one. Well, the restaurant was sorry but it was fresh out. So that's when this skindiver guy comes over to the table. I don't know whether he'd heard us or not, but the next thing you know, he goes flying over to the pier and heaves himself into the water, and I'll be goddamned if he doesn't come up with one of those loup fishes on the end of his spear! "Voilà, babe! Compliments of Stokely Carmichael, the Honorable Martin Luther King and Cab Calloway." Well, it really was a kind of charming thing to do. I mean the way he presented the damned thing. Anyway, we bought him a drink, dinner. He didn't say much except that even as a kid he'd always had these strong lungs.

(*Goes up to* FROGMAN'S *image on screen, shouts.*)

Come on out you son of a bitch. I'll take you on even if you have got strong lungs and I am a little afraid of that spear gun.

(*Climbs down as though nothing happened.*)

Well, actually, he didn't seem like a bad guy. We didn't know anybody… So the next thing I know, Jeannie and I are in Cannes again and I find myself saying "Let's go see old Scuba Duba." All my own idea. I have to say that for Jeannie. So far she hadn't even taken a good look at him. I was the mastermind – really brilliant the way I served him up, just like a bowl of strawberries. The way I planned it, a real Normandy Invasion. I smoked him out that second time. It wasn't easy – he was out working on shrimp boats or something – but I found him and for the next week we just went around together. I even took him along when we went to get her hair set.

(*Rips out one of the slides and tears it up.*)

One thing I resent is paying for all those drinks, you bastard, and this has nothing to do with your being black, so don't get any ideas.

(*Closes up slide equipment.*)

So next thing I know, she insists on being by herself one afternoon, and then a second time, a few more times, and then I get this call earlier tonight. This is it, she says. I'm with him, I'm staying with him and it isn't just for tonight, it's for always, words and music by Irving Berlin. I can go down to the Mediterranean and drain it out cup by cup as far as she's concerned and it's not going to do any good. I'm supposed to stay with the children and maybe she'll call and at a certain point she'll come and get them because she wants them. And she's not kidding either, this really *is* it. You should have heard her voice. So what am I supposed to do now, ask this guy if I can come visit my kids once in a while? Work my ass off so she can buy gold flippers for a goddamned frogman? What's he gonna do, send my kids to some spade frogman school? A spade underwater school in France somewhere?

(*In mock imitation.*)

"Now you take the flippers in one hand…" What am I supposed to do, start calling up girls now and ask them out on picnics? In the condition I'm in? What do I do, go to Over Twenty-eight dances? I mean, what the hell am I supposed to do? I'm shaking like a leaf. How do you feel about men crying?

MISS JANUS   It's all right. I don't have any special theories on it. I have a feeling it would be all right if you did it.

HAROLD   I'll just turn around here for a second and try to get it over with as soon as possible.

(*Turns head.*)

That ought to do it. It wasn't too bad, was it?

MISS JANUS   You have a beautiful neck.

HAROLD   Really? It's big, but I never thought much about it being beautiful. What a nice thing to say. I mean, if you said I was handsome that's one thing, but when you compliment a neck you've got to be serious.

MISS JANUS   What happened then?

HAROLD   Maybe I ought to show it off a little more.

(*Switches.*)

Well, first I thought I'd get her back by insulting him. "You think you're going to be able to shop at Bendel's on what he makes with those flippers? What do you think is down at the bottom of that French ocean anyway? There's just a bunch of French shit down there. And back in the States, what'll you do, go to Freedom Marches together? And back in the States, sit around and read back issues of *Ebony*?" Well, I didn't get very far with that approach. So then I switched over to all the things we'd had together over the eight years, and you know I couldn't come up with very much. The sex you can forget about. You see, one time, when we were just married, she looked up while we were making love and saw my hand up in the air. "What's that?" she asked. "It's my hand," I said. "Well, what's it *doing* up there?" she asked. "Where's it supposed to be?" I asked. "Well, shouldn't it be *doing* something?" she said. Well, I said, the other hand was *doing* something, but she didn't see it that way and it was kind of downhill ever since then. Now the only time she gets excited is in bathrooms at other people's houses.

MISS JANUS

I never tried that. I'm not knocking it or anything. But it's funny.

HAROLD

Yeah. She goes into the toilet and she pulls me in there with her and she's as hot as a snake. All our friends know by now. We go to a party, they all stand around waiting for us to come out. Believe me, that's no sex life. So I tried to think of some other stuff and all I could come up with was a trip to Quebec we once took. "What about that trip to Quebec?" I said to her. "What about it?" she said. "Well, wasn't it something?" "It wasn't that great," she said. I said, "Yeah, but didn't we see a ship from Israel at the waterfront that wasn't even supposed to be there?" She agreed we saw a ship from Israel, but that was no reason to keep a marriage together. I had to agree with her there. So then there wasn't much else I could do except hit her with the kids. Well, this Negro gentleman friend of hers was way ahead of me on that. He told her the kids were going to be fine, she said. Yeah. "Well, maybe that's in coloured divorces," I said, "but my kids aren't going to be fine.

(*Hollering out window.*)

Not with any goddamned spade frogman stepfather." I love my kids. I have this one game I play with them. I got to show you. It's called "Can't Get Out."

MISS JANUS   What do I do?

HAROLD   Oh, just pretend you're Jamie. I say to you "Now I'm going to get you in one of the toughest grips known to the Western World. It's called the 'Double Reverse Panther Bear Pretzel Twist.' No man in history has ever been known to get out of this grip. Are you ready? Do you dare to allow me to get you into it?"

MISS JANUS   I do.

HAROLD   I do, Daddy.

MISS JANUS   I do, Daddy.

HAROLD   Well, then I spend a long time getting them into it. This kind of thing.

(*Twists her around, this way and that, tying up her arms, legs.*)

"Okay," I say, "now you're in it. No man in history has ever broken out of it." Then I let them twist around for a while and gradually I let them slide out and I say "Good God, the first man in history ever to work his way out of the Double Reverse Panther Bear Pretzel Twist! Congratulations."

(SHE *has made no effort to get out, stays twisted.*)

MISS JANUS But I can't get out.

(HAROLD *kisses* MISS JANUS *awkwardly, then ardently, then tenderly.*)

HAROLD (*Setting her down.*)

Look, that isn't why I told you about the game. I wasn't working around to that, or anything.

MISS JANUS It's a lovely game.

HAROLD The kids love it. They can play it with me for hours.

(*As an afterthought.*)

Listen, what kind of a kiss was that? I just don't know how good I'd be at kissing under the circumstances.

MISS JANUS It was delicious. Listen, I don't want you to get the wrong idea. I've done an awful lot of drifting in and out of things, but actually I've only really had one all-out start-to-finish love thing. A writer. We were both very new with each other. What we did was wander through each other like we were the first man and woman. The sex part with him was always very quick, almost instantaneous. It was very sad. We're still friends. He married a girl who's as quick as he is—and he says they're very happy.

HAROLD Maybe I'll get through the night. I've got this great fighting chance... I once read a novel about a guy who just got divorced and what he did to get through was a lot of physical activity. Push-ups. Every morning he'd get up, light a fire, and start doing push-ups. I wonder if I ought to try a few.

(*Gets down on the floor and begins doing push-ups, gets up to around ten.*)

You know, it's not bad at all. I wonder how deep knee bends would be.

(*Does a few.*)

Hey, you know it's really something. I'll be goddamned if it doesn't help.

(*Starts to do an isometric exercise.*)

I'll probably come up with a hernia.

MISS JANUS   Hercules had a hernia.

HAROLD   Hercules? How'd you find that out?

MISS JANUS   I saw a statue of him in the Louvre and there was a funny little hernia line nobody else noticed. I once told a boy I had a hernia. At college. He drove me out to a lake and asked me how I'd feel about some heavy petting. It sounded so *heavy*. So I told him I had a hernia... Listen, would you like a massage?

HAROLD   (*With irony.*)

Yeah, that's exactly what I'm in the mood for. I'm supposed to drift into a little massage...

MISS JANUS   You know, a lot of people believe it's a homosexual thing. I don't. But I don't even believe homosexual relations really exist. Certainly not between two men.

Why would they bother? There are so many other things they could be out doing. I don't think it's ever really happened. Maybe in Germany once or twice, in the thirties, but that was the only time. I think it's something someone made up to play a big joke on society. A couple of fags made it up.

HAROLD

You know, for a second I thought that frogman was a fag. He's probably been keeping it up his sleeve. I just remembered something about the way he slithered into the water after that fish.

(*Reflecting.*)

That's all I'd need. Losing my wife to a goddamned fag.

(*Quiet, desperate anger.*)

Boy, if I ever found that out, then I'd *really* break his head....

(*In a different mood.*)

I'm not sure I want to know, but where'd you learn about massages?

MISS JANUS

My father taught me how to do them. I thought it would be incestuous, but it really isn't. It just felt good.

HAROLD

How do you know it's not incestuous?

MISS JANUS

With my *father*?

HAROLD

What do I do?

MISS JANUS

Roll up your pants.

HAROLD

What do you mean?

MISS JANUS

I want to do your knees.

HAROLD	What good's that going to do?
MISS JANUS	You'll see.
	(HAROLD *rolls up his pants.*)
	They're very attractive.
HAROLD	Thank you.
	(SHE *begins to massage his knees.*)
MISS JANUS	(*Still massaging.*)
	I bet you were good in sports too.
HAROLD	I was about average. But I always had great form.
	(*Demonstrating with scythe.*)
	I'd pick up a tennis racket or start fooling around with a basketball and I'd make these sly little moves and these great championship faces and they'd think God knows what was coming. I did a lot of losing, but it didn't seem to matter.
	(*Responding to massage.*)
	Hey, you know, you're right – it *is* good. Of all things, I never even knew I *had* knees before and yet here they are, out of the clear blue skies, feeling great.
MISS JANUS	I believe some people have a special touch, don't you? That young man in the French movie who all he has to do is touch this girl on the wrist at a party and she moves right out on her millionaire husband and goes to live with him in a little cellar somewhere. And it all started with a touch.
HAROLD	(*Pushing* HER *off.*)

I'd like to make a little announcement about my knees. My knees have just become the greatest knees in town. Everyone said they were finished, washed up, that they'd never work again. Well, you've put them back on their feet. I want to thank you for giving them another break in show business.

(THEY *shake hands.*)

But she never showed up, did she? And nothing's really changed, has it? ... Dr. Schoenfeld.

(HE *picks up phone, dials.*)

Dr. Schoenfeld?

(*Cut-out of* DR. SCHOENFELD *appears.*)

SCHOENFELD'S VOICE	Speaking...
HAROLD	Surprise. This is Harold Wonder. I'm in Cap Ferrat.
SCHOENFELD'S VOICE	All right, if you want to be in France. I didn't realize you knew I was here.
HAROLD	Oh sure. Don't you remember? In that clothing store? We were both trying on clothes. Look, I'm in terrible trouble and I'm just calling up guys. But this isn't just a call. I really have to ask you to come over here. You can make it in about twenty minutes. Look, obviously you don't *have* to come...
SCHOENFELD'S VOICE	What's the difficulty, Harold?
HAROLD	The difficulty is that I'm climbing up the walls. It's the kind of thing you'd never get into in a million years. It's

my wife. She's out with this goddamned frogman and I think she's going to stay the whole night. It's that whole night thing that scares me.

SCHOENFELD'S
VOICE   Harold, isn't the frogman just one chapter?

HAROLD   One chapter? Oh yeah, and I've been turning him into the whole Modern Library. Look, Dr. Schoenfeld, I don't want to appear ungrateful, but that capsule style just isn't enough this time. Can you come over? I've tried everything. A little while ago I started to shake. I'm afraid I'm going to blow sky high. I don't want the kids to see me that way. So could you please try to make a run over here? Please.

SCHOENFELD'S
VOICE   Harold, you know what your problem is – you're good at looking up and down but you've never once looked at life sideways.

HAROLD   Look, Doc, I don't want sideways now. Will you... don't give me sideways.

SCHOENFELD'S
VOICE   No sideways, eh?

HAROLD   No. I really need you. Could you sort of come over and spend the night? I really need somebody I can depend on.

SCHOENFELD'S
VOICE   Well, Harold, I have a friend visiting.

HAROLD   There's plenty of room. Bring your friend along. I really do need you, right this second.

(HE *hangs up*.)

(DR. SCHOENFELD'S *cut-out disappears.*)

He'll be here. I know it. If it was me and I heard a guy who sounded like I did, I'd be over in a flash.... You know, right this second, as we sit here, my wife is up on a chandelier with a spade.

MISS JANUS   You like the way that sounds, don't you?

HAROLD   What do you mean? Spade? I guess so. It comes out so smooth. They have all the good names.

(*Enunciating very deliberately.*)

Coon. Shine. All those n's. Wop. Kike. See? Nothing. If you ask me, I think she picked one of them just to confuse me. Or to prove something to me. She knows how mixed up I am about coloured guys. There's just no right way to be about Negroes. I went down to that Freedom March a couple of years ago in Washington. All of a sudden. Actually I knew I was going, but I like to tell it as though I made up my mind on the spur of the moment. Makes me sound like more of a sympathizer. Anyway, I got down there and when the marching started it got kind of crowded and a man fainted. I stopped to see if I could help and a huge Negro in back twisted my arm up behind me and said "Pass 'em by, pass 'em by." He kept walking me that way till we got way the hell out in a field somewhere. And he's still saying, "Pass 'em right up, pass 'em by." Finally I said "I passed the son of a bitch by already," but he just kept marching me along saying "You ain't really passed him all the way by yet." He finally let me go, I don't know where, someplace in Baltimore. That didn't exactly put me in the right mood for a Freedom March. I got to listen to some of the speeches anyhow – they've really got some wonderful speakers, guys you've never heard of who can knock you out of your seat.

MISS JANUS   And then something terrible happened, right?

HAROLD   You ready?

MISS JANUS   *Clunk.*

                    (SHE *does a fastening thing at her waist, then explains.*)

                    Safety belt.

HAROLD   Well, I'm listening to the Reverend and he's really going to town. All goose bumps, really nailing the thing down, right in front of the Lincoln Memorial, the most stirring thing you ever heard. About a third of the way through I start to look at this little coloured Freedom Marcher type. She had one of those behinds you can balance things on. I couldn't take my eyes off her. I felt rotten – right in the middle of this stirring thing and I can't get my eyes off her ass. So I kind of get close to her and before long we start kidding around – in whispers – and next thing you know I've got her behind a tree. I couldn't stop myself. She was a little laundress girl from Delaware who came down by bus – her name was Eurethra – we didn't talk much. Anyway, what I'm leading up to is right through this Reverend's speech – one of the most brilliant addresses ever given – I read it next day in the *Times* – there we were, me and Eurethra behind the tree. Hell, maybe it was her fault as much as mine. I mean she was the coloured one. *She* really should have been listening. I mean, what kind of guy does such a thing?

MISS JANUS   A very warm, glandular human being.

HAROLD   That'll be the day.

(*Goes to shutters and cries out.*)

Jeannie…

(*Then changes his mind.*)

I'm not going to do that any more. Listen, what do you want anyway? You enjoy listening to a messed-up guy?

MISS JANUS	I don't know what I want. Right now I'd settle for a guarantee that I'm never going to be hairy.
HAROLD	Hairy?!
MISS JANUS	Like Janine Harper, a girl in my home town. She was a beautiful redheaded girl and then one summer she got very hairy. Turned into Neanderthal Man right there before everyone's eyes. She cleared up in the fall and I guess she's all right now – I hear she married an optometrist – but I never got over it. If I could just be sure that'll never happen to me. If I could have a written certificate, something I could carry around. I just don't want to have to spend a hairy summer.
HAROLD	Well, *I'll* guarantee it. It'll never happen to you. Never in a million years.
MISS JANUS	And I've decided that I'd like to go to bed with you.
HAROLD	Me, you'd like to go to bed with? Oh you crazy kid.
MISS JANUS	Listen, your wife has raced off with another man and you can't adjust to it. That's not an everyday thing, you know. It's not as though you were carrying on about urban renewal. Besides, I'd like to see what it would be like. With many men you just know, but with you…
HAROLD	I'll tell you what it's like. With me, it's a one-handed number.

(*Changing tones.*)

That black bastard told us he's got beautiful paintings on the wall. I can just about imagine. I can just picture the shit he's got hanging up there. Haven't you heard? That's where Picasso is having all his shows these days. At that guy's apartment. The second Picasso knocks off a canvas he rushes it over there, special delivery. It's the only place he'll show his paintings. Maybe he likes the smell up there; it really brings out the values.

(*Phone rings.* HE *looks at her apologetically, lets it ring, goes to phone, looks back and then takes it near a clothing closet, where, standing up,* HE *begins to pull coats over his head for privacy.*)

Hello-Jeannie-and-if-it-is-don't-say-a-word-because-I'm-doing-all-the-talking. Now Jeannie, look, I don't care what's happened. You got a little nervous, it's a foreign country, all right, I'm a little shook up, but it's over, I forgive you, and you're coming right the hell home where you belong. We'll take a few trips. Remember, we were going to use this as home base and see Barcelona? ...It is *not* just the beginning! ...All right then, we'll go to Liverpool. Any place you say... I'm the one who *is* facing facts! ...Jeannie, I'm all alone here. What do you think this has been like for me? ...A *strain?* ...You're holed up with a coloured frogman and you call me up and all it is is a little strain... Strain?

(*Goes to window, yells.*)

I'll give you a strain, you fuckin' Mau-Mau. I'll strain your ass.

(*Back to phone.*)

I'm not trying to put him down… All right, all right…
Okay, he *is*. He's very nice. Nicer than I'll ever be…
Listen, I've been plenty nice, in my own style… I use
both hands too! It was just that one time. I can't explain
it.

(*Hardening.*)

Now listen, Jeannie, you get your tail the hell back here
or I'm throwing you right the hell out of the house. You
hear? I don't care if you're impressed or not…. All right,
you're out. You hear that? I've thrown you out of the
house…. I don't have to have you here to throw out of
the house. You're out.

(*Pacifying.*)

All right, Jeannie, I know. I'm sorry. Okay, if you say it's
real – you say it's honest – then that's what it is. That's
right, baby, with us it was filth and with your new friend
it's purity all the way… I know… Uh-huh. That's right,
baby. Will you put your clothes on now and get your
white ass over here. What do you have to do, get one
more of those screws? One more of those little screwba
dewbas? Got to feel those Freedom Flippers around
your toochies one more time? … Jeannie, I can't make
it through the night… Jeannie, you're not home in
an hour, I swear to Christ I'm walking the hell out of
here… I don't give a shit about the kids… That's how I
feel about it. I don't see you in the doorway, I'm walking
right the hell out of here into the French night… You
just try me…

(*Soft.*)

Jeannie, do you remember Quebec? All right, forget Quebec. I'll never mention it again. I mean, just come home. Will you just do that... He won't *let* you?

(*Out the window.*)

You won't let her, you bastard. I just heard about that. It just came in over the wire. What do you mean, you won't let her? You open those goddamned doors or I'm coming over there to cut your balls off.

(*To the phone.*)

All right, I'm calm... I am... It's because you can't see me. I'm in complete control of myself.

(THIEF *enters, pot on his head, and begins to steal things.* HAROLD *doesn't see him.* MISS JANUS *tries to warn* HAROLD, *then to reason with* THIEF.)

(HAROLD S*houts out the window.*)

You like my billboards, eh? I'll give you billboards. I'll billboard your ass when I get hold of you, you black son of a bitch.

(*Into phone at same time he spots* THIEF.)

Yeah, well he can afford to be a gentleman. I'll show him dignity. I'll show him who's beneath who. Now, Jeannie, will you just come home.

(*Hollering out window, ignoring* THIEF.)

You went one step too far. A lot of guys make that mistake with me.

(*To* THIEF.)

Hold on a second.

(*Into phone.*)

Hold on a second.

(*Picks up scythe and as* THIEF *leaps through window hurls it after* HIM *through the shutters, then plumps down in a chair, addressing* MISS JANUS *with great casualness.*)

She'll be here in twenty minutes flat. Have I steered you wrong once tonight?

(BOTH *watch curtain come down.*)

CURTAIN

ACT II

(THE ACTION CONTINUES DIRECTLY FROM ACT I.)

MISS JANUS   You were wonderful. I never saw anyone move that fast.

HAROLD   I love action. That's the one thing I'm crazy about.

(*Door knock.*)

That's my wife. I know her knock.

(GENDARME *enters holding* THIEF'S *arm with one hand, scythe with the other.*)

GENDARME   I'm sure you must have some explanation, monsieur.

HAROLD   Hey, you got him! That's great!

GENDARME   (*Taking out notebook.*)

Just because you Americans have everything and we have nothing does not mean you can make fun of me.

HAROLD   Who's making fun? Where's the fun?

(*To* MISS JANUS.)

Was I just making fun of him?

GENDARME   Never mind. Do not take that superior tone with me. And then as soon as I leave, the sly little jokes will begin. Just because you have your washing machines and your General Motors.

HAROLD

Look, I don't want to go into a whole thing. Will you just book this guy and get him the hell out of here?

THIEF

All men are thieves.

GENDARME

He is not entirely wrong, you know. I arrive here, you expect me to fall at your foot, to lick your boot. France is a proud nation, monsieur, something you and your General Motors will never understand.

(*Pauses.*)

What is the salary of the American policeman?

MISS JANUS

Sixty-three hundred dollars a year.

(HAROLD *is astonished.*)

It was in the *U.S. News* and *World Report*. I just happen to remember.

GENDARME

(*To* THIEF.)

I, Pierre Luclos, am paid forty-two francs a week and on top of that, these Americans come here and throw shit in my face!

HAROLD

(*Imitating Jack Benny.*)

Now wait a minute!

(LANDLADY *enters.*)

LANDLADY

(*Surveying scene.*)

It has not happened here. I saw nothing. It did not occur in my house. Oh perhaps once, when the Russians were having their Yalta conference in the attic. They are terrible, the Russians. You know how long I know the Khrushchev boys? I would never have them in my house again.

HAROLD

Tonight I'm getting Yalta? I need a little Yalta?

GENDARME

Hold the hose, monsieur. I am not one of your Negroes that you can trample…

HAROLD

Listen, that problem is not quite as bad as it sounds. Some of them are doing pretty well. Pretty goddamned well.

THIEF

All men are thieves. The butcher is a thief. The baker. The honest man who works at the same job for forty years, from nine to six, goes home each night to his family and never steals a dime. What is he? A thief. He is cheating his loved ones. He is cheating his destiny. He is a lowly rotten scum of a thief, the worst of them all. There you have philosophy.

HAROLD

There you have garbage.

(*To* GENDARME.)

Are you going to lock this guy up or am I supposed to wait till he kills a few of my kids?

GENDARME

When I am ready, monsieur, and only when I am ready.

(*Paces the room elaborately.*)

The charges, Mr. Yankee Doodle?

HAROLD

What do I know about French charges? Ask him why he wears that pot while you're at it.

THIEF

Decadence, sir. A symbol of your rotten, bourgeois Western decadence.

(GENDARME, *choked with emotion, begins to sing* "*La Marseillaise.*" THIEF, LANDLADY *and* MISS JANUS *join him while baffled* HAROLD *looks on.*)

GENDARME   Come, my friends. We have taken enough from this man.

THIEF   (*Banging pot on his head.*)

All men are thieves. Murderers, liars, and pederasts too. I offer you philosophy.

(THIEF, GENDARME, LANDLADY *exit, all singing* "*La Marseillaise.*" DR. SCHOENFELD *enters. He appears to have weekend baggage with him. He is dressed, atypically, in a very flashy manner.*)

HAROLD   Dr. Schoenfeld! What a pleasure. Let me take your bags. It's amazing, I feel better already.

SCHOENFELD   Good evening, Harold.

HAROLD   Didn't you bring your friend?

(CHEYENNE *appears.*)

CHEYENNE   Here I am, love. 'Ello there. Say, Phillsy told me about your wife. Never you mind. Soon as she runs out of money that spade'll drop her like a hot pizza.

HAROLD   Good Christ!

SCHOENFELD   Harold, I'd like you to meet Cheyenne.

(*Noticing* MISS JANUS.)

I don't think I've had the pleasure.

MISS JANUS   Hi, Dr. Schoenfeld, I'm Carol Janus.

CHEYENNE   'Ello lamb chop, how are you?

HAROLD   (*Privately, to* SCHOENFELD.)

This is the fancy treatment you thought up? My wife's out screwing the rules committee of SNICK and you had to come running over here with this?

SCHOENFELD   It's just one chapter.

CHEYENNE   (*At bookshelves.*)

Say, you got any books by Bernie Malamud? Once you get started on those urban Jews it's like eating potato chips. If you ask me, you can take C. P. Snow and shove him up your keester.

SCHOENFELD   Cheyenne, please. I have something important to say to Mr. Wonder.

(*Beckoning* HAROLD *toward couch.* MISS JANUS, CHEYENNE *sit on couch, too.*)

Harold, it's become obvious that we can't work with sideways any longer. Perhaps it's time we looked into our relationship. Now, I agree we've had some good times in the clothing store. But you know, you've never really taken our talks seriously. Do you know why, Harold? Because they've never really cost you anything.

HAROLD   Cost me anything...

MISS JANUS   Oh sure, it's just like figs. You know how delicious they are. But imagine, if you had all the figs in the world, they just wouldn't be delicious any more.

HAROLD   Look, hold the figs. Go ahead, Dr. Schoenfeld.

SCHOENFELD   Your friend is right. What I want you to do, before we go any further, is to give me something valuable—not money—but something you really treasure. Then I'm convinced you'll listen to me.

CHEYENNE   (*With pride, to* MISS JANUS.)

He's my shrink, you know.

HAROLD   (*Looking around.*)

Something valuable…what kind of valuable?

MISS JANUS   I didn't know they dated patients.

(HAROLD *exits in his search.*)

CHEYENNE   (*To* MISS JANUS.)

We don't start the couch bit until after the fall. This is sort of a trial period. Like exhibition baseball. Say, you've got an honest face. Shall I tell you what my problem is? Sexual climaxes.

MISS JANUS   You poor thing.

CHEYENNE   No, no, I have too many of them. He's going to try to cut me down to just five a night.

MISS JANUS   Oh, that should be plenty.

(HAROLD *returns.*)

HAROLD   All I could find was this muffler. My mom knitted it for me when I was around ten. There was a deaf kid who tried to take it away from me once – a strong deaf kid, a deaf bully. I had to hit him right in the mouth. It was no fun hitting a deaf guy, believe me. But it was worth it. I got it back and I've kept it ever since.

SCHOENFELD   Now you're really sure you care about this muffler?

HAROLD   I really do.

SCHOENFELD   All right, give me the muffler. Now, Harold, listen very carefully. When I was in the Army, I was in grain supply. As a matter of fact, I was the officer in charge of purchasing barley for the entire states of Kansas and Oklahoma. Now barley, God bless it, as we all know, gets very damp. And damp barley means only one thing – trouble – not for the barley, but for the barley personnel. Well, sure enough, I soon came down with a respiratory ailment. Now, the Army doctors were convinced it was a rare disease common only to barley workers. Do you know what it turned out to be, Harold? It wasn't a barley disease at all. It was bronchitis.... Harold, do you see what I'm getting at?

HAROLD   (*Muses awhile.*)

Give me back the muffler.

SCHOENFELD   You're not getting the muffler back.

HAROLD   Come on, hand it over.

SCHOENFELD   No, Harold.

HAROLD   Give me the goddamned muffler.

(*Tug of war follows, with* MISS JANUS *and* CHEYENNE *joining in.* HAROLD *gets muffler back. Winding muffler around his neck.*)

Y'ain't not getting the muffler. Not for barley. I was better off with sideways.

SCHOENFELD   (*Collecting himself, gathering dignity.*)

Well, Harold, it's a little late. Perhaps in the morning you'll see things differently.

(*Standing beside* CHEYENNE.)

And now, if you'll show us to my room…

(*Gathers luggage.*)

HAROLD   Room? Yeah, that's right, I forgot. All right, go ahead. Go upstairs. Take a left at the top. Make sure it's a left. I got my kids up there.

MISS JANUS   Good night, Dr. Schoenfeld. 'Night, Cheyenne.

CHEYENNE   Nighty night, all.

SCHOENFELD   (*At top of stairs.*)

I don't need his muffler. It was for his own good.

CHEYENNE   C'mon love, let's have a go.

(THEY *enter bedroom.*)

HAROLD   How long have I known that guy? Now he's giving me barley.

MISS JANUS   He really let you down, didn't he?

HAROLD   No, it just seems that way to the untutored eye.

MISS JANUS   Maybe you'd like to hear about my obscene phone call.

HAROLD   Nope. I don't know much tonight, but that's one thing I'm sure of, that I don't want to hear about your obscene phone call. Maybe when this whole thing dies down we can meet somewhere and you can tell me about it. At some little French place. I just know I'm not up to it tonight… How obscene was it?

MISS JANUS   That's the whole point. It was the most timid obscene call in the world. It was from a boy at Columbia. He was studying library management and I think he'd been reading Henry Miller. He called me from the stacks. It was the shyest obscene phone call. So I asked him to meet me in the school cafeteria…

(CHEYENNE *appears in robe.*)

CHEYENNE

Listen, is there a crapper in this joint?

HAROLD

(*Gesturing.*)

Oh man.

CHEYENNE

(*Walking toward indicated room.*)

I hope it has a bidet. I've been all over France and I'm the only one who hasn't seen one yet. I'm not even sure I'm looking for the right thing.

(*Disappears in room.*)

HAROLD

Why'd you have to meet him? Why'd you have to meet him and then come here to France and tell me about it with what I'm going through? Why didn't you just hang up?

MISS JANUS

His face was practically all horn-rimmed glasses. I talked to him for hours. It was his first obscene phone call, just like it was mine. We went up to my room for a while…

HAROLD

All right, all right, hold the punchline. I knew I didn't want to hear this one. And I was right.

(CHEYENNE *appears in underwear, soaked.*)

CHEYENNE

Well, I'll be goddamned. So that's how it works. You'd think they'd at least have directions on the little stinker.

(SHE *goes back into the bedroom.*)

HAROLD

(*To* MISS JANUS.)

Why didn't you call the police? That's what you're supposed to do. If everyone just invited perverts over to the house for tea like that what the hell kind of a world would it be? ... Probably wouldn't be that bad.

(*Reflecting.*)

Jesus, I just remembered. I made one of those calls myself.

MISS JANUS   Listen, more people than you think...

HAROLD   No, I was just a kid. I had a crush on a teacher named Miss Baines, so I looked up this word in the dictionary and I said it to her. "Hello, Miss Baines," I said. "Yes," she answered. "Pelvis," I said, and then I slammed down the phone. I think she knew though. Every time I got up to recite, she put on this pelvic expression. That's something to remember, here in France, years later, and my wife's on a trapeze with the Brown Bomber...

(CHEYENNE *comes downstairs humming, semi-nude.*)

CHEYENNE   Hi. Phillsy likes to have a little warm milk before he gets rolling. Helps him crank up his motor. Y'know, I knew a bloke once who liked me to cover him up from head to toe with mayonnaise. Poor bastard. It was the only way he could get his rocks off.

(CHEYENNE, *erupting in vulgar laughter, enters kitchen.*)

HAROLD   You want to know something *really* awful?

MISS JANUS   What's that?

HAROLD   I think I know where to find them.

MISS JANUS   Your wife?

HAROLD   Remember her? That's really something to have to come right out and admit. Eleven Rue Domergue – he said it one night and it stuck with me. So how come I'm not going anywhere? How come I'm just hollering out of windows?

MISS JANUS   You're just not ready.

HAROLD   When do I get ready? When she moves to the Congo?

                 (CHEYENNE *comes out of kitchen, whistling. Goes back into bedroom.*)

MISS JANUS   (*Stretching.*)

                 You know, it isn't that much…. We could just sort of drift upstairs too…

HAROLD   (*Getting up.*)

                 I don't know how it would be…. Maybe if you just told me a few more of those stories. Do you have any left? Just feed me a few more and we'll see what happens.

MISS JANUS   All right.

                 (SHE *comes toward him, sits behind him.*)

                 Once I was trying on dresses in a store up in Maine. I reached into the size nine rack and there was a little man all covered up inside a two-piece jersey ensemble…

                 (*Light changes as though many hours have passed. Indication is that it is dawn.* HAROLD *is still in his bathrobe, groggy, exhausted.* MISS JANUS *has been going on with her stories, as though* SHE *has been telling them endlessly.*)

…a Russian take-out restaurant. Anyway, I was delivering an order of borscht to a customer and I see his pockets are all filled with petitions, bills, proclamations. So I put two and two together and I said "Listen, just because you're in the House of Representatives doesn't mean I'm staying over tonight."

(*Realizes how much time has gone by.*)

Oh my God, I locked Nero and Abby out.

(SHE *exits.* MRS. WONDER *appears, rather forlorn at the moment, and prone to bumping into things. She is gentle in manner.*)

JEAN WONDER	Harold… How are you?
HAROLD	What do I know?
JEAN	How are the kids?
HAROLD	They're fine, under the circumstances. You all right?
JEAN	Pretty good. My arm hurts though.
HAROLD	What happened?
JEAN	I think I got gas in it.
HAROLD	What do you mean gas? You can't have gas in your arm.
JEAN	No, that's what it is. I'm sure of it. Somehow it curled around through here and up around here and got right into my arm. It'll be all right.
HAROLD	It's not gas. Remember that party? What was it, Friends of the Middle East? You were positive you were having a heart attack. *That* was gas.

JEAN   That was a small heart attack, Harold. I just accepted it and when it was over I was grateful and that was the end of it.

HAROLD   Everything else all right?

JEAN   My neck is a little tensed up. I'm just going to have to live with that.

              (SHE *starts to dust.*)

              You okay?

HAROLD   Jeannie, don't dust now, will you?

JEAN   Well, what am I supposed to do, leave it there, just let it accumulate? Breathe it all in? Foreign dust. How do we know what's in it?

HAROLD   There's nothing in it. It's just a little French dust. No dusting now, okay? Will you do me that favour? I'm starting to get a little sore. There's something that happens to your shoulders – when you dust – and I don't want to get involved in that now. They get frail or something. I probably never told you, but I can't stand to see you dust. It's like I took this young, fragrant, hopeful, beautiful young girl and turned her into an old cleaning lady.

JEAN   Women like to dust, silly. It doesn't hurt them.

HAROLD   Well it hurts the hell out of me. I can't stand it.

              (SHE *stops dusting.*)

JEAN   How about you? In your bathrobe. Can I stand that? And making that face at me…

HAROLD   Which one's that?

JEAN	You know which one. There's only one. You made it at Gloria Novak's wedding reception the first time I ever saw you. At the salad table. I look up from my salad and I see this big guy making a face at me.
HAROLD	I don't know what you're talking about.
JEAN	Not much. That little boy face. Whenever you want something. Look at you. You can't even switch off to another one, even right now. You did it to me then and you're doing it right now.
HAROLD	What I'm doing right this second, right now?
JEAN	That's right.
HAROLD	I never made this face before in my life.
JEAN	Right. I just came in here... I was going to get a few things...
	(*Starts for bedroom.*)
HAROLD	(*Intercepting her.*)
	No things, no things. That's one line I never want to hear.
	(*In British accent.*)
	"Dudley, I've come for my things." Anybody gets their things, that's the end of their things. In this house you get your *stuff*, hear? And you don't get that either.... This is some mess.
JEAN	I know.
HAROLD	I think this is the worst we ever had.

JEAN

I don't know, Harold. I think when I was pregnant and we couldn't get any heat in the apartment and you had to organize a warmth committee in the building at four in the morning. I think that was worse.

HAROLD

No, I think this is worse. I had a lot of people on my side in that one. I had the whole building cheering me on. I'm all alone on this one.

JEAN

What do you mean? Do you think I love this? That I love every second of it?

HAROLD

You're loving it more than I am. Anybody'd be loving it more than I am. There's not one person I can think of who wouldn't be loving this more than I am…. You think we'll get out of it?

JEAN

I don't know, Harold. At this point I'd settle for just getting through the morning.

HAROLD

(*On his knees, cracking.*)

Ah come on, Pidge, will you just quit it right now? Will you get the hell back home? Will you just stay here? What do you want to do, ship me off to Happydale? I'm down here on the floor. I'm not a guy who does that.

JEAN

(*Comforting.*)

I know, Harold, I know.

HAROLD

(*Recovering slightly.*)

Look, there's just one thing I have to find out. This is important. Did you get into things like Pidge? Does he know I call you Pidge?

JEAN

Is that what you consider important? Is that what this is all about to you? Pidge?

HAROLD   No, seriously, I just have to know that one thing and then I'll never bother you again.

JEAN   I may have said something…

HAROLD   (*Leaping up in triumph.*)

You told him Pidge. That's probably the first thing you blurted out. I was just on the floor where I've never been in my life – and you had to tell him Pidge. I was just hoping you'd keep one thing separate, one little private area so that maybe we could start battling our way back, inch by inch, to being a little bit together again. What you did is just fork it right over…

JEAN   I don't remember if I told him…

HAROLD   (*Not hearing her.*)

All right, number one, cancel what I just did on the floor. And number two, drag in that chocolate shithead. I've been waiting for this all night.

JEAN   Harold, could you try to be a little dignified. I can get that style from my father. I don't need it from you. I grew up with that. You know, for a second I really felt a little something – the first time in years – and then you have just heaved it right out the window.

HAROLD   (*Peering through window.*)

Is he out there?

JEAN   Yes, he's out there, Harold.

(*Sarcastically.*)

But you can't see him because it's still a little dark and he has all this natural camouflage.

HAROLD	(*Still looking out.*)
	Very funny. How come he's afraid to get his black ass in here?
JEAN	He couldn't possibly face you, Harold. Not after what I told him. You see, I told him about your poise. About your quiet dignity. About your finesse in handling difficult situations. He wouldn't come within ten miles of the place.
HAROLD	I'm going to be dignified. I'm going to be Dag Fucking Hammarskjold. Just get the son of a bitch in here.
JEAN	Harold, will you just listen for a second? I'm not going to ask for your full attention because I know I'm not entitled to that. Not in the short span of time that's been allotted to me on earth. But will you listen a little? I've been outside…
HAROLD	I don't know you've been outside? I don't have it engraved in my brain for all time – that you've been out there?
JEAN	All right, you know I've been outside, Harold. But what you don't know is that I looked around a little. And I saw what they're doing out there. They're not hollering out of windows, Harold. They're not taking their families three thousand miles to a beautiful new country with dozens of charming little villages to roam around in – so they can stand around in bathrobes and shout things out of windows, and never see those charming villages.
HAROLD	Look, you want to know the truth? I've been trying not to say this, but you're forcing it out of me. All right, here it comes. I just don't happen to think those villages are charming. You want me to say they're charming,

all right, they're charming. You got what you want. But they're not that goddamned charming. They act charming. No one's ever questioned it before, so they get away with it. You take Lexington Avenue and fix it up a little and you've got the same charm. And it didn't cost you thirty grand to get over here.

JEAN   Harold, let's face it. We both know there's only one charming thing in the world. You…in your bathrobe… shouting out of windows. That's the entire list. The charm line up of our generation…. Let me tell you what happens to me when I'm outside, Harold. The strangest thing. You know how I trip a lot and bang my head on things and we both think it's cute, although actually it's very serious and some of the injuries will probably turn malignant at a future date – well I don't trip over things out there. I didn't bang myself on the head once.

HAROLD   You were supposed to get your eyes checked, Jeannie. What happened to that? Is that what you were doing out there in the bushes – with that guy – getting your eyes checked?

JEAN   There's nothing wrong with my eyes, Harold. I wish it were that. If it were an eye problem, believe me, I'd grab it. No, there's a reason that women out there don't bang into things and kill themselves. You see, they've had a breakthrough out there, Harold. They actually – and you'd better sit down for this one – they actually believe there's a difference between men and women. And here's the shocker of the year. You ready? They're doing something about it. They've come up with a separate way of treating women. They speak a little more gently to them. They actually say things to women – romantic things. And it doesn't make them feel like Herbert Marshall either.

HAROLD	Look Jeannie, we've talked about this... Once and for all, I can't say "Your eyes are like deep pools" unless I really believe they are a little like deep pools. Even then I can't say it.
JEAN	They don't have that trouble, Harold. They say things that are beyond your wildest imaginings. Do you know they even recite poetry to women.
HAROLD	That miserable two-bit coon recites poetry... All right, get him in here. (FROGMAN *enters casually.* HAROLD *walks through door and doesn't see him.*)
HAROLD	(*Shouting.*) I dare you to come in here and face me. (*Spots* FROGMAN.) I'm sorry, I got a little confused.
FROGMAN	(*In a heightened, mocking laying-it-on-thick Negro style. This "put-on" approach continues throughout – with only one exception, indicated further on.*) That's all right, sweetie-baby, it's a tough scene all around. I can tell you got a lot of heart.
HAROLD	Now look, I'm cold, I'm shaky, I've been up all night. I'm not at my best in the morning. It takes me till around noon to hit my stride. To be perfectly frank, I'm a little afraid of people. It's a completely irrational thing. Little girls, even old ladies. I have this feeling they were all in the Golden Gloves once. You know what I mean?
FROGMAN	Let me give you a little advice, Jim. You sass an old lady, she gon' lean back and give you the bad eye. She gon'

work some roots on you, babe, then you really in a shit storm.

HAROLD   Very cute, very cute. There's just one thing. We happen to be on *my* turf now, you son of a bitch...

                 (*Using scythe,* HAROLD *begins to square off with spear gun-carrying* FROGMAN.)

                 (REDDINGTON *enters.*)

REDDINGTON   Hi, Pidge.

HAROLD   Pidge! Everybody knows Pidge. Who the hell is this?

REDDINGTON   Is everything all right...

                 (*With glance at* HAROLD.)

                 Pidge?

JEAN   I'll just be another minute.

FROGMAN   Hey baby, you made the scene just in time. We all gonna sit down and have some chitlins.

REDDINGTON   Cool it, Foxtrot.

HAROLD   Oh, now we're getting a little "cool it." How about a little "daddy." A little "dig," a little "daddy." Who is this guy, Jeannie?

JEAN   Harold, this is Ambrose Reddington.

HAROLD   That tells me a lot.

JEAN   Harold, I'm sorry, I really wanted to avoid this. I met Ambrose a few days ago... A complete accident. He was very sweet to me and I take full credit for him. Foxtrot is your idea, one hundred per cent. A Harold Wonder special. You like him, you can't live without him? I'll tell

	you what – pick up the phone, make a reservation and the two of you can go flying down to Rio.
HAROLD	Hilarious.
FROGMAN	Suppose I just slip into my travelin' duds…
HAROLD	(*Threatening.*)

Don't push me too far, just don't push me too far.

(*Recovering.*)

Give me a minute to adjust to this.

(*Contemplates.*)

I can't adjust to this.

(*Walks toward* REDDINGTON. *Resuming anger.*)

As I was just saying.

(*Shouts.*)

We're on my turf now, you son of a bitch. We're not at any Black Muslim convention.

FROGMAN	Oh I see where it's at.
HAROLD	(*To* FROGMAN.)

Look, I'm sorry to have to use the racial stuff, but you'll just have to overlook it. It gives me a slight edge, but I can assure you it's got nothing to do with my true feelings. If everyone felt the way I did, you guys would have clear sailing from here on in…

(*To* REDDINGTON, *shouting.*)

What's important is that I can still smell my wife on you, you bastard.

REDDINGTON	Mr. Wonder, I can see that this is a difficult situation for you, but we certainly ought to be able to deal with it as mature adults.
FROGMAN	He ain't gonna be one of them mature adults. He gonna fetch the debbil on that poor old man. He gonna read around there and work some roots. Right on that poor black rascal's head. Whooooooeeeee.
HAROLD	Very cute, very cute.
FROGMAN	Shame on you, babe. Just 'cause that poor old man went out there in the bushes and jugged your wife a few times...
HAROLD	Now you watch *your* ass. Just because I was wrong about you doesn't mean I was wrong about you.
FROGMAN	Shame on you, man. For shame...

(REDDINGTON *starts to cough*.)

JEAN	Oh my God, are you all right?
REDDINGTON	It'll pass. It's nothing.
JEAN	(*To* HAROLD.) Now look what you did.
HAROLD	What *I* did!
JEAN	You started his cough. Will you do something useful for a change? Where did we put the Cheracol?
HAROLD	Cheracol? You want me to nurse him back to health? It's in the medicine cabinet. Oh never mind, I'll get it.

(*As* HE *fumbles in the drawer*.)

I really have to congratulate you, Jeannie. I mean a little affair is one thing. But the entire Harlem Globetrotters. That's really style.

FROGMAN

Hey, Ambrose. What'd you need this shit for? You could have stayed out there in the car.

REDDINGTON

I couldn't allow Jean to face this alone.

(HAROLD *picks up medicine bottle, carries it to* REDDINGTON *and pours a spoonful.*)

HAROLD

I'm not enjoying this, you know. I'm not enjoying it one bit. I don't even know why I'm doing it. I guess that all it amounts to really

(*As* REDDINGTON *swallows medicine.*)

is that I'm helping a guy with a bad cough.

(LANDLADY *and* TOURIST *enter.* LANDLADY *spots* FROGMAN *and runs toward him exultantly.*)

LANDLADY

Sidney… How marvelous. It is Sidney Poitier.

(*Embracing* HIM. *Then taking in frogman get-up.*)

You are in a James Bond movie. I can tell… How come you don't write your friend, you naughty boy?

FROGMAN

I got jammed up at the Cannes Film Festival. Once you get up there on top, everybody wants a slice of the action. You got producers tryin' to get tight with you. You got them starlets…

LANDLADY

Ah, you rascal.

(SHE *has unintentionally stepped on one of his flippers.* HE *points this out and she backs away with a blush.*)

TOURIST	I got nothing against you people. What the hell, a party's a party. I'd sit around with a goddamned Yugoslav if I had to. Wouldn't blink an eyelash. I always say, if you keep alert you can even learn something from a Slav. Long as that Slav understands that when the buzzer rings I head back to my section of town and he gets up and goes back to his *Slav* side of town.
HAROLD	(*To* TOURIST.)
	I really don't need any help from you.
FROGMAN	(*In mock defence of* TOURIST.)
	Hey, don't pick on him. That's my man. Anyone mess with my man gotta hit on me first, babe.
	(*Confidentially, with arm around* TOURIST.)
	You like to meet some nice black chicks?
TOURIST	Well actually, I'm just down here for a few weeks…
FROGMAN	I mean some really groovy chicks. I don't mean any of that street trash. Something real high class…
	(TOURIST, *abashed, exits.* LANDLADY *follows him.*)
HAROLD	Jeannie, what do you want to see, a stretcher case? A French nervous breakdown? You're going to get one, you know. I'm going to sail into one any second now.
FROGMAN	Baby, you just not getting the message. You heard about those neighbourhoods that get moved in on and there's nothing you can do? You're just not facing facts. You the neighbourhood in this case, babe.
REDDINGTON	Foxtrot, please. Mr. Wonder, I'm sorry that my friend feels it necessary to behave in this fashion, but if you'll

permit me—I'm afraid he has made a valid point. Realistically speaking, your wife and I have formed a powerful attraction for one another. It has enormous meaning to both of us. It began quite innocently, I assure you.

HAROLD

I know about those innocent attractions. I could hear the bedsprings creaking all the way across the Mediterranean.

REDDINGTON

Mr. Wonder, that's not very groovy of you.

(LANDLADY *and* TOURIST *enter.*)

TOURIST

(*To* LANDLADY.)

I sort of like the French. It's the Italians you got to watch. The important thing is to keep them away from shiny stuff – rings, silverware, tinfoil. Drives 'em crazy. It isn't anything they can help. Something happens inside their heads. Any time you invite an Italian person over, make sure you don't have anything around that makes a jingling sound.

(LANDLADY *and* TOURIST *go upstairs on inspection tour.*)

HAROLD

Do you actually have to handle him, Jeannie? Right in front of me. You know, if I didn't see this, maybe in thirty-three years or so I might be able to forget the thing, pretend it didn't happen... Jeannie, will you do me a favour? Will you name one way in which this is helping me? One way that it's enriching my life...

FROGMAN

You just not taking the right attitude, man. You could clean up. I heard about this fella, he hired another guy to jug his wife and then he sold tickets to his buddies to come down and watch. You work it that way, at least you pickin' up a little cash on the deal. Tell you what. Here's my money, I'll take five tickets down front, right now...

TOURIST   I've been watching you awhile, Foxtrot, and I just want to say right now that I respect you as a man. You're coming through loud, clear, and nasty and I can hear you. Now I'm white and you're one of those black guys, but just one man to another – me standing here, you standing way the hell over there...

FROGMAN   I respect you too, man. I'm going to give you something. I'm going to give you a shine. I'm gonna shine up your ass. Hey, shine 'em up, shine 'em up.

             (*Chases* TOURIST *out.*)

LANDLADY   (*Wagging finger.*)

             Sidney!

             (LANDLADY *exits.*)

HAROLD   (*To* REDDINGTON.)

             If you were a Puerto Rican I'd feel the exact same way. I'm just using every weapon I can lay my hands on.

REDDINGTON   When one's masculinity is being threatened, one often resorts to...

HAROLD   One? What kind of one? Who talks like that? Is that the kind of poetry he recites? One. Jeannie, you know I've followed you on a lot of this, and I admit I don't walk off with the award for the Greatest Married Fellow, but I honestly don't see the big deal about this guy.

REDDINGTON   (*Reciting, in something of a counterattacking style.*)

"What matter cakes or wine or tasty bouillabaisse...
When love lies bruised and clotted on the thin and
punished lips of our American black dream..."

HAROLD Big deal. LeRoi Jones, right?

REDDINGTON No. I wrote it.

HAROLD I'd like to see you get that junk published.

REDDINGTON I've already heard from the *Partisan Review*.

HAROLD (*Panicked.*)

The *Partisan*? What did they say?

REDDINGTON They were impressed by the combination of raw power
and delicacy...

HAROLD Hah! You don't even know a standard *Partisan*
rejection... "Dear Sir: Despite the raw power and
delicacy of your poem, we regret..."

REDDINGTON No, they bought it. It's scheduled for the fall issue.

HAROLD Oh well, the fall issue...

JEAN Harold, you could learn a little from this instead of
automatically hating it.

HAROLD Learn? All right, I'm learning. Here's a little poetry

(*In a lisping, effete style.*)

"Intruders ye be...make haste, abandon this place...
Or I'll punch that spade in his coloured face."

REDDINGTON (*With controlled anger.*)

Don't push me too far, mister.

HAROLD (*To* REDDINGTON.)

Push you too far... The main thing is I can outwrite you, I can outfight you, I can outthink you...

FROGMAN   Yeah, but there's one thing you can't out him, babe. That man there

(*With a sly, sexual gesture.*)

is a coloured man.

REDDINGTON   Foxtrot...

FROGMAN   Yeah, baby.

REDDINGTON   I see no point in turning this into a gutter confrontation.

FROGMAN   Shit man, I was just holdin' up my Negritude. That man was hittin' up on you, Ambrose.

(TOURIST *and* LANDLADY *enter.*)

REDDINGTON   I can take care of myself.

HAROLD   Well, what the hell would you do? I mean, say you were in my shoes. Say I was you for a second and you were me.

FROGMAN   You askin' an awful lot, babe.

HAROLD   No, I'm serious. What the hell am I supposed to do? Let your friend just waltz off with her? Throw in a few kids, maybe some General Electric stock I've been saving up to show I'm not prejudice. You know this is not an easy position to be in. I'm just trying to hang in there. It's bad enough I'm not allowed to get as angry as I'd like. If I toss in a little racial slur every now and then, you'll just have to put up with it. If you don't like it, you know where the door is.

(HE *suddenly grabs a wine bottle and smashes it on a ledge, brandishing the jagged edge toward the* GROUP, *the* NEGROES *in particular.*)

All right, that's it. There's no more problem because I just solved the whole thing. Anybody comes near me they get my initials carved in their head.

(*Everyone freezes in real panic and shock as* HAROLD *grabs* JEAN, *brandishing jadded bottle with great menace.*)

I can't go through with the thing.

(*Flings away bottle.* FROGMAN *catches it.*)

REDDINGTON   (*Putting out arm.*)

Jean... It's all right, Pidge, it's all right.

FROGMAN   (*To* HAROLD.)

You know I like that – the way you whipped out that bottle and almost cut your own natural-born ass off. I liked that, man. Little more of that, you gonna be ready for One Hundred and Twenty-fifth Street.

TOURIST   Say, you fellows aren't serious about that Black Power thing, are you?

FROGMAN   You'll be the first to know, babe. We got you right at the top of the mailing list.

(*Chases* TOURIST *out with jungle sounds and spear gun.*)

HAROLD   Look, Jeannie, I really don't want this happening right now. If you'd come in here last night when I was fresh, rested, enthusiastic, when I was at the top of my form, you'd have seen a whole different guy. I'd have settled this thing in two seconds flat and believe me everyone in this room would have walked out of here feeling like a complete winner. But, Jeannie, I can't operate in the morning, you know that. I haven't even settled into the day yet. I'm still in my bathrobe. You put me in a pair of slacks, you'll see a whole different scene. I don't even have my eyes open and you're throwing spades at me – a whole blizzard of spades. Spades – as far as the eye can see...

REDDINGTON   Mr. Wonder, please, a little self-control...

HAROLD   All right, all right. I just want you to know that I'm not entirely responsible. There's something about mornings. I assure you if it was last night you wouldn't have heard a single racial slur out of me. Maybe one or two, tops.

(*To* REDDINGTON.)

Now look, you got her, all right. You sneaked in there, you read poems, you did crazy things, I don't know what you did. Whatever it was, the main thing is she's yours. For the next thirty-two years she's going to be strapped to your side. At the most maybe I'll bump into her accidentally one night, have a little drink, maybe some dinner. It'll be different then. Neither of us will talk much, just as though we're total strangers. Maybe our fingers will touch accidentally, and we may even slip off to a motel together and have this exquisite evening, just as though it were choreographed, everything that happens just sheer magic. And then we part at dawn, a little sadly, perhaps, but without any real regret.

LANDLADY   (*Simultaneously with last part of* HAROLD'S *romantic fantasy, timed so that last word of her speech and* HAROLD'S *come together.*)

Ah, l'amour. The joy of it. The tears and the heartache. When there was only one person in the world for you. The secret meetings. The touch of a hand in the darkness. Ah, when I was a jeune fille. Floop, floop, floop.

HAROLD   Will you floop the hell out of here? Look, can I please have a couple of minutes alone with my wife? Can we empty out Grand Central for a while?

JEAN   Harold, there's nothing we can't say right out here…

REDDINGTON   Pidge, I think it's a reasonable request. But if you'd like me to stay here, I will.

JEAN   No, it's all right.

REDDINGTON   (*Reciting in a soothing manner.*)

"Wait here and I'll be back, though the hours divide, and the city streets, perplexed perverse, delay my hurrying footsteps…"

LANDLADY   (*To* REDDINGTON. SHE *is still angered by* HAROLD'S *rough words.*)

Take care, monsieur. Eddie Fisher has stood in this very room and played the exact same trick on Elizabeth Taylor.

(LANDLADY *exits.*)

REDDINGTON   Come on, Foxtrot.

(HE *enters kitchen,* FOXTROT *lingering slightly behind.*)

HAROLD   (*To* FOXTROT.)

Now look, can I just have a few minutes to wind up the marriage.

FROGMAN	You got any cornbread in the kitchen?
JEAN	Once and for all, will you stop putting him on, Foxtrot?
HAROLD	He can ask for cornbread. What's wrong with that? I don't happen to have any cornbread, but he can certainly ask for it.
FROGMAN	(*Straight, no accent, serious.*)

I was born on a farm in Aiken, South Carolina, one of nine children, six boys and three girls. They called me Billy-boy in those days because no matter what happened, I'd just buck my way through. Once I was driving and I turned a car over seven times, got out, kept walking to the post office. I stay close to one brother, George, who sees to it that I don't wise off. He says "Maybe you're great, but let other people find it out. Don't you tell them." I lost my father on a farm accident, and didn't care much about it one way or the other. My mom's still pretty. She won a contest designing hats and my brother told the newspapermen if any of them interviewed her he'd go after them and kill them no matter where they tried to hide… I haven't got tired of the water yet. Nothing much to it. I'll just stick with it, make a few bucks, probably quit sometime.

(HE *shuffles off.*)

HAROLD	What? Boy, what a pleasure to have two seconds of peace in your own home.
JEAN	All right, Harold, what's the great thing that you had to have me all alone to tell me about?
HAROLD	C'mon, Pidge.

(*Spitting.*)

Ptuuii. I can't even call you Pidge any more. I'll have to think up a whole new name.

JEAN

Will you stop, Harold. You're hurting my hip.

HAROLD

What do you mean? I'm not touching you.

JEAN

When you act a certain way. It goes right to my hip. I've told you that a thousand times, but you never listen.

HAROLD

All right, I promise never to say anything that'll hurt your hip.

(*Soft again.*)

Look, Jeannie, I've seen him now. I've checked out his routine. Truthfully – what has he got? What do you want, coloured? All right, here.

(*Breaks into an elaborate shuffling dance routine in the old Bill Robinson style.*)

And that's without even *being* black. It's better that way. You don't have any of the headaches. You skip the aggravation. All you have is the flashy stuff.

JEAN

(*Somewhat amused.*)

I can't laugh, Harold. It'll start the whole sinus thing and I can't afford that now.

HAROLD

Jeannie, I know the guy now. He's not in my head, he was just *in* here. I mean, what *is* he? He's coloured and he coughs. Is that what you want? That's what you're giving me up for? A coloured cougher.

JEAN

(*Jumping up.*)

All right, there's one. You wanted an example – that's one, right there. The last thing you said is the kind of remark that's complete death to my hip. You might as well take a hammer and just pound on it right here.

HAROLD   All right, all right, you made your point. I just want to sit here one more minute, quietly, and wind up the marriage. The whole marriage that I thought was like a rock and would last a thousand years – a whole British Empire of a marriage.

(THEY *rest a moment, silently.*)

All right, what does he do?

JEAN   What do you mean?

HAROLD   You know what I mean, Jeannie. You know. He's a coloured guy, he knows stuff, he does stuff, they teach him things. Give me an idea.

JEAN   Oh God. He doesn't do any *one* thing, Harold. People don't do *one* thing. It's a whole lot of things, if you must know. A whole collection of things.

HAROLD   Well what are they? Can you tell me a few?

JEAN   You're really going about this the wrong way.

HAROLD   Tell me just one – one thing.

JEAN   I can't.

HAROLD   Will you come on, one lousy thing. What do you have to lose?

JEAN   I can't *do* that.

HAROLD   Jeannie, for crying out loud, the marriage is down the drain. I'm sitting here, I'm a terminal marriage fellow, will you tell me one thing?

JEAN	He strokes my ear…
HAROLD	(*Leaping up.*)
	I can't do that? I can't outstroke that son of a bitch twenty times a day? I can't outearstroke him? Let me show you.
	(HE *fights to stroke her ear.* SHE *struggles.*)
	There you are – stroke…stroke…stroke.
JEAN	(*Throwing him off.*)
	Harold!
HAROLD	There. All right, how was it?
JEAN	It was thrilling, Harold. It really turned me on. Can I go now?
HAROLD	A coloured stroke is great, huh, but if I do the identical thing, the exact same stroke, it's nothing. A Caucasian nothing. In the dark you wouldn't have known one from the other.
JEAN	You almost pulled my ear off.
	(HAROLD *clutches her suddenly, tries to make love to her.* SHE *struggles against him.*)
HAROLD	Jeannie, look, I never felt this way. I don't know what just happened to me…some kind of crazy new feeling…
JEAN	Harold, will you please…there are people here…we're not in the bathroom…
HAROLD	(*Continuing.*)
	I don't care where we are.

JEAN	Harold, you know I can't just do that – just leap into it...and you haven't said a word to me. A preliminary word...
HAROLD	(*Stops embrace.*)
	All right, all right...Jeannie...you've got some helluva pair of tits on you...
	(*Jumps on her again.*)
	You want hands? A lot of hands? You couldn't live without them. Here's hands – forty-two hands.
JEAN	Harold!
	(SHE *throws him off again after great struggle.*)
HAROLD	(*With wounded dignity.*)
	All right, will you just go now? Will you just collect your coloured friends and stop taking up my valuable time?
JEAN	I've been trying to, Harold. I've been trying to leave. But you've been stroking my ear.
HAROLD	Well you had your last stroke from your old marriage. Your last broken-down, second-rate, technically lousy stroke. I just want to prepare you for something, Jeannie. So you don't hear about it second hand. So you don't read about it in the *Harlem Bugle*. When you walk out of here, I'm not folding my tent...
JEAN	Well I don't want you to, Harold. Is that what you think would make me happy – tent-folding?
HAROLD	What you don't see is that beneath all these layers of what you consider weakness – and maybe I'll even

agree with you a little there – there's another layer that you don't know anything about. It's a little weak too, but it's toughly weak. That's the strongest kind. It's a great layer that comes from way back in my family – little villages in Budapest where these peasants would ride through the village brimming over with this tough weakness. How old am I? I've still got thirty-five good years to go. I'm a young guy. I've got great knees. I've got a terrific neck. Something you never noticed.

JEAN

I've noticed it, Harold. Many is the time I've found myself just sitting and staring out of windows, thinking about your neck. I just never could put my feelings into words. Can I go now?

HAROLD

Who's keeping you? Have I said one word? All right, a parting salute. To you I'm like an old tattered issue of *National Geographic*, right? That's how you see me. Something you find in a closet. One of those terrible issues from around 1936 with all those pictures of Borneo peasant women with those long, endless Borneo bazooms. And I remind you of one of those issues. Are we agreed on that?

JEAN

Are we agreed on *what*?

HAROLD

But we're agreed on that, right? That I'm this old discarded guy that no woman under ninety-five would take a second look at. Oh, maybe there's a girl somewhere who's come up with a rare disease, been in a few airplane wrecks, couple of oven explosions. If the thing were set up very carefully in advance, a girl like that might sit down and have a drink with me. But aside from that type, I'm dead, right? It's all over? We agreed? Okay. What if I said I could produce – voilà! Right here in the middle of this fascinating French floor, before your very eyes, a young, beautiful, fascinating girl who tells stories that if the *Partisan Review* ever knew about them they'd have a man over here with a contract by six o'clock tonight... I mean *good* stories, Jeannie, I don't mean that cakes and bouillabaisse shit. All right, now you take that gorgeous girl, I don't think she's out of her teens yet—if she never saw a spade in her life she wouldn't blink an eye—you take that girl, with a figure that I don't even want to get started on, a whole new kind of body for the mid-nineteen sixties, take her and imagine her in this château trying every trick in the book—and believe me, Jeannie, these new girls coming up have got plenty of new routines—this gorgeous sylph-like girl trying every trick in the book to get your husband—who supposedly doesn't know the first thing about handling ears—to get *your* husband into the hay with her. All right. What is that? A little fictional tidbit? A little bouillabaisse? Would you like to meet her right now?

JEAN   Did you meet her, Harold?

HAROLD   You're damned right I did.

JEAN   Well I think one member of the family is enough.

(*Starts to leave.*)

HAROLD   (*Calls through window.*)

Miss Janus...

(*Then, for* JEAN'S *benefit.*)

Carol...Honey.

MISS JANUS'S
VOICE   Yes?

| HAROLD | Can you come over for a second? I want you to settle a little argument. |

| MISS JANUS'S VOICE | Be right there. |

| HAROLD | (*To* JEAN.) |

All right, hold still one second and you're going to see a little cornbread. You're going to see the monstrous fate that awaits your husband as soon as you take one step outside. The reason your husband has to get down on his knees and beg you not to go.

(MISS JANUS *enters*.)

Voilà!

| MISS JANUS | Oh hi. We had a little accident. One of Nero's sculptures fell on top of him. It's a giant carving of a dead Spanish peasant who was sitting in the stands during a bullfight and got fatally gored by accident. Nero was going to present it to the Spanish government. He was positive Franco would go wild when he heard about it. |

| JEAN | Is your friend all right? |

| MISS JANUS | Oh yes. Luckily he's on a grease kick now. He thinks that if people keep themselves greased up as much as possible, it'll help them slide by some of their problems. Anyway, we just slid him out from under the dead peasant. You must be Mrs. Wonder. |

| JEAN | Yes. And Harold's been reading me your dossier. You're very pretty. |

| MISS JANUS | He told me all about you too, Mrs. Wonder. You're very attractive. You have this sort of mid-sixties look. No matter what I do to myself I can never look that way. |

JEAN	Thank you. I've been feeling kind of mid-fifties tonight. Oh my God!
MISS JANUS	Is anything wrong?
JEAN	Do you realize that I have walked this coastline from end to end looking for printed slacks like that? Did you buy them here?
MISS JANUS	In town. Right here in Cap Ferrat. Listen, do you think they fit? Tell me, really. Every time I try something on, I've got this pack of girls from Düsseldorf who swoop down and tell me I'm making the mistake of my life.
JEAN	They fit, they fit. Listen, with your figure…
MISS JANUS	*My* figure. Listen, have you looked at yourself lately? I have a marine biologist friend – if he saw you, believe me, you'd never get out of his office alive.
HAROLD	All right, time out. That's it. Hold it right there. What is this, roommates at Radcliffe? It's supposed to be a tense confrontation. Where's the tense? If it can't be tense, I don't need it. I got other things to do.
	(SCHOENFELD *and* CHEYENNE, *fully dressed, with luggage, come out of bedroom and make way downstairs.*)
JEAN	Oh, he's been here too. My husband's friend, the Dean of American Mental Health.
MISS JANUS	Oh, I know Dr. Schoenfeld. Hi, Dr. Schoenfeld. Hi, Cheyenne.
SCHOENFELD	(*Opening door.*)
	Harold, you're on your own. I can't carry you any longer. It's time you got up on your own two feet and faked your way into the adult community.

(*Exits with* CHEYENNE. FROGMAN *comes out of kitchen.*)

FROGMAN

(*To* JEAN.)

What's shakin', baby? You 'bout ready to split? Let me call Ambrose so we can get goin'.

HAROLD

(*To* MISS JANUS.)

My wife's interviewing gospel singers. She's got thirty more of them out in the kitchen.

MISS JANUS

He's putting me on.

FROGMAN

No, no, he ain't putting you on.

(*Sings "Uncle Misery".*)

I don't get no visits from my
Uncle Josh or Uncle John.
And even Uncle Andy stay away from my door.
The only uncle who ever come aroun'…

(HAROLD *joins.*)

Is my Uncle Misery.
Uncle Misery
Uncle Misery…
I didn't invite you here…
He say "I know son,
I don't need no invitation"…

(*Stops singing, leaves* HAROLD *trapped in song and hand-clapping.*)

Sheeeeet…

JEAN

Foxtrot, aren't you laying it on a little thick?

HAROLD	Don't talk to him that way, Jeannie. The man enjoys singing. Let him sing a little. What's so terrible? He's not hurting anybody.

(*To* FROGMAN.)

C'mon let's sing it again. I love that song.

JEAN	(*To* MISS JANUS.)

Harold, the Great Defender of the Negro, the black man's best friend. You should see him driving. Get the picture. We're in the car on the highway and a black person in the next lane has just gotten a little too close and forced us off the highway. Harold doesn't know it was a black man yet and so he's gotten out on the road in his traditional style and is trying to round up ten men for a firing squad. But then Harold sees it was a black driver. And then we have our ceremony. Harold reaches into the other car and kisses the driver on both cheeks. For being a coloured driver, and for being nice enough to force us off the road.

HAROLD	Boy, you sure can lay it on thick, Jeannie. Just 'cause you've got an audience. You know damned well I've straightened out plenty of coloured guys. I just don't do it in front of you. I've taken on whole moving vans full of them.
JEAN	I can just about imagine.
HAROLD	I *don't* straighten out coloured guys? You're going to stick to that, right?

(*Punches* FROGMAN *in the jaw, knocking him down.*)

All right, there! I just straightened one out.

MISS JANUS *hides behind a couch*

JEAN   (*Running to* FROGMAN.)

Good Christ, Harold...

(HAROLD *is dancing up and down in his bathrobe, fighter style.* TOURIST *and* LANDLADY *enter.*)

TOURIST   I saw that, son. That's the only language they understand.

(HAROLD *punches* TOURIST *in jaw.* TOURIST *reels out door into* LANDLADY'S *arms.* REDDINGTON *runs in from kitchen.*)

REDDINGTON   What's going on here?

(HE *grabs* HAROLD, *immobilizes him.*)

Mr. Wonder, control yourself.

HAROLD   Jesus, what the hell did I do?

(*To* FROGMAN.)

Look, I'm really sorry. I just realized what happened. Will you accept my apology? I honestly didn't mean to do that.

FROGMAN   (*Into fake mike, imitating Joe Louis.*)

I want to say hello to my folks in South Carolina, I want to say hello. He hit very hard with his left hand, he very strong with his left hand. I want to say hello. And I want to say hello...

HAROLD   All right, cut it out.

MISS JANUS   Maybe if I massaged his shoulders...

HAROLD   It won't be necessary...

(*Disparagingly.*)

Jesus, I really handled that beautifully.

REDDINGTON	Come on, Pidge, let's go.
JEAN	I'll be back for the children.
REDDINGTON	Mr. Wonder, I've had my fill of this vulgar exhibition. I find it truly regrettable that you couldn't have accepted this in a more gentlemanly fashion. You've blown your cool, Mr. Wonder, and you are far from a credit to your race.
HAROLD	Jeannie, please, no doors, okay? No doors. I'm not fooling around anymore. You leave now, you might as well sign a death certificate for me. Just fill one out and leave it over there on the couch on your way out. Jeannie, I'm about to come out with the worst thing a guy ever said in the whole history of modern recorded statements. The kind of thing that if I knew I was going to be reduced to saying it, I wouldn't have even bothered growing up. Jeannie, I have to have you in the house. And you can do whatever the hell you want. Just so long as you're here. You have to have coloured guys, you got 'em. Take them upstairs with you. Close the door, I'll make the goddamned beds for you. You want a trapeze, I'll set that up too. Anything you want. I just need to have you here awhile. So I can slowly build up my strength. You want to leave then, we have a whole new situation.

(*To* NEGROES.)

Look, what do you guys have to lose? You're coughing your head off; *you* can hardly stand on your feet. Where you going to get a cab at this hour? You go upstairs with her, it's cool, it's comfortable, you got television, you got everything you want…

JEAN	Will somebody get me out of here? Right this second.
REDDINGTON	Jean.

(*JEAN* takes REDDINGTON *by the arm.*)

HAROLD	(*To* JEAN *on her way out.*)

What did I just do? I was trying to be nice to them. Well, what am I supposed to do, throw them out on their ass? Punch them in the mouth – I did that already...

(*JEAN and* TWO NEGROES *exit.*)

(*Calling through door.*)

These people haven't had it that easy, Jeannie. They haven't had any sleigh ride. We tend to forget. They've done plenty of suffering...

(*Also through door.*)

Jeannie! Where you going? Hey, can't you guys get your own broads? Wait till I get my hands on you...You black bastards...What the hell did I do? Did you see me make one wrong move? Did I step out of line once? She'll be back. She just needs a few days in the sun – a different kind of sun. We get crummy sun right here around the house. You sit out there for hours, you end up white as a sheet.

MISS JANUS	You know, I think you're right. I think I'm whiter than when I started.
HAROLD	What the hell am I supposed to do now? I'm a lonely guy.
MISS JANUS	Oh, it's because she's just left. I used to feel the same way at Camp Winnetkawonta in the Berkshires when

my parents just dumped me there and drove off. But then as soon as I got involved in the activities – the second I got out there on the archery court…

HAROLD

Look, please, don't tell me archery. It's an entirely different situation. I'm some lonely guy. I've been on my own how long…

(*Checks watch.*)

Look at that, four minutes and I'm a lonely guy. Maybe if I got out of here. Listen, do you have anything on? Something where I can really celebrate being this free guy? This unattached winner…

MISS JANUS

I told Abby and Nero I'd help them look for shells tonight, just before it gets dark. You could come along, if you don't mind Nero being a little greasy.

HAROLD

Who minds? I'm not going to mind. Long as I get out of here. Long as I get started in my new life.

MISS JANUS

Okay, I'll tell them. I don't like to just spring things on Nero. I like to give him plenty of lead time…. You be okay?

HAROLD

I'll be great. I just have to get through till around three o'clock in the afternoon. If I can just do that, I'll be in the best shape of my life.

MISS JANUS

See you later.

(SHE *leaves.*)

HAROLD

(*Running to window.*)

Hey, you'll be there, won't you?

MISS JANUS

(*Returning.*)

Of course.

(SHE *kisses him on cheek, exits.*)

HAROLD Well don't worry about it. If you can't make it, put it out of your mind. Either way is okay.

(*Pause.* HE *paces back and forth, picks up scythe, looks at it, flings it aside, can't seem to get comfortable. Recreates all activities he's tried throughout evening—calls, knee bends, etc., everything that's worked for him—but he cuts off each one in the middle. Running to door, shouting.*)

Jeannie, I'm going out with broads—two of them. We're going to look for shells. You met one, remember? Her friend's even better looking – there's no comparison. You see this new girl, you forget the other one's alive... I'm going out with the two of them. And this greasy guy—he's coming along too...

(HE *turns away for an instant, then returns to window as lights dim.*)

Once I go looking for shells, that's the last word you'll ever hear from me. If I find out I love it, I'll throw you right out of the house. Right out of the house. You hear me, Jeannie!

(*Lights go to black.*)

Right out of the goddamned house.

CURTAIN

CHARACTER LIST

OLDTIMER — A grey-haired hunched man lounging comfortably in a towel.

TANDY — A young man (35 to 45), slightly puzzled by his surroundings.

BIEBERMAN — An attractive fellow.

MEREDITH — A very blonde beautiful young girl, wearing a sheet.

ATTENDANT — A Puerto Rican man.

GOTTLIEB — Attendant's assistant, who also plays the part of a bartender in Act II.

WHEELCHAIRED MAN — The man is in a wheelchair; his legs, braced, are completely useless. He wears steel-rimmed glasses and his neck, too, is coiled in a brace, as though he has been in a whiplash accident.

GIRL DANCER — A young, pretty girl in a short skirt.

FLANDERS — A detective, with a gun in hand.

ADDITIONAL CAST — Two young men, Broker, Longshoreman.

ACT I

A STEAMROOM   (*Benches or slabs and a single overhead shower. Effect of
steam is achieved by either steam or light or both. People
speak, disappear in the haze, re-appear. Characters are
costumed in sheets or cloths. At the beginning of the action,*
TANDY *sits downbeside* OLDTIMER. TANDY *is ever
so slightly puzzled by his surroundings but does his best to
conceal this mild concern. He has a great deal of trouble
when he makes contact with the hot seat.*)

OLDTIMER   That's really something, isn't it, when you sit down?

TANDY   It's a bitch.

OLDTIMER   It don't bother me. When you're a young fellow it
bothers you, but then you develop a tough ass.

TANDY   I knew your beard got tough, but I didn't realize the
other thing…

OLDTIMER   It's true.

(THEY *sit awhile.*)

I've had some wonderful sweats in my time.

TANDY   That right?

OLDTIMER   Oh yeah. When the Polish came in, the union gave them a steambath down on Fulton Street... Nobody sweats like the Polish... What you're doing now...

TANDY   (*Feeling himself.*)

                Yes?

OLDTIMER   That's garbage. You're not sweatin'... I never exercised much, though. You see this area here.

                (*Pulls flesh in his lower back region.*)

                I always wanted to keep that nice and soft in case I got some spinal trouble. So the needle could go right in. I know guys, athletes, they're so hard you can't stick a needle into them... I figure it's a good idea to keep it soft back there.

                (THEY *sit awhile longer.*)

                How do you feel about heart attacks?

TANDY   I'm against them.

OLDTIMER   Lot of people are. I'll say this for them, though, they don't mark you on the outside. They leave you clean as a whistle. That's more than you can say for a gall bladder.

TANDY   I agree with you there.

OLDTIMER   I seen guys get cut up for ulcers, they got bellies look like the map of downtown Newark, New Jersey... People have always been a little too rough on heart attacks. The heart attack's always gotten a raw deal.

                (BIEBERMAN, *concealed behind a pillar, clears his throat and then spits on the floor.*)

Hey I saw that.

BIEBERMAN   What?

OLDTIMER   You know what. What you did. Expectorating like that. It's disgusting.

BIEBERMAN   What's wrong? It's a natural fluid.

OLDTIMER   You're a disgrace.

(*To* TANDY.)

You got to watch him like a hawk. Probably farting back there, too. Who the hell would ever know in a steambath?

BIEBERMAN   (*Still concealed.*)

I heard that. I'm not farting.

OLDTIMER   Congratulations...

BIEBERMAN   My generation doesn't do that.

OLDTIMER   Your generation can kiss my ass.

(*To* TANDY.)

What's your line, young fella?

TANDY   I just quit my job. I was teaching art appreciation over at the Police Academy.

OLDTIMER   That right? What the hell... I guess you got to do something. Police, eh? Ever notice how you never get any trouble from the good people?

TANDY   Well, that's for sure.

OLDTIMER	It's the bad ones you got to watch. You run the bad ones off the street that'll be the end of your crime. You got a son?
TANDY	No, I've got a little girl.
OLDTIMER	You got a son, I hope he's a drunk. That'll keep him off drugs. He starts in on that
	dope stuff you can kiss his ass goodbye.
	(*In reference to* BIEBERMAN.)
	What's that guy doing now?
TANDY	(*Checking behind pillar.*)
	Looks like he's eating an orange.
OLDTIMER	Yeah, but what's he doing?
TANDY	(*Checks again, gets hit by a fusillade of pits.*)
	He's spitting out the pits.
OLDTIMER	Stupid mother.
	(*Shouting to* BIEBERMAN.)
	Hey knock it off, will you?
BIEBERMAN	Well what am I supposed to do with them?
OLDTIMER	Hold them in your hand, swallow them, shove them up your ass – what do I care? Just don't spit them out. Didn't you ever hear of a person tripping on pits?
	(*To* TANDY.)
	They get some crowd in here. He's probably a fag, too.
TWO YOUNG MEN	(*Invisible, speaking in unison.*)

No, we're the fags.

OLDTIMER

I beg your pardon.

(*More or less to himself.*)

I knew there were fags in here.

(*To* TANDY.)

You broke a sweat yet, son?

TANDY

I can feel one coming.

OLDTIMER

You know what would go down really well now? A nice cool brew.

(*A* BAR BOY *enters with two cold beers and glasses. In later appearances, he is referred to as* GOTTLIEB. TANDY *and the* OLDTIMER *each take a beer and begin to sip at it.*)

I drank a lot of beer in my time. One thing I'll say for myself is that I never gained weight. I gained bloat. The trouble is – bloat weighs a lot too. Most people don't realize that. Bloat can kill you.

TANDY

What do you do?

OLDTIMER

I done a lot of things. In my late years I took to hackin' a cab. I was terrific once I got my daily icebreaker. But until then I wasn't fit to live with. That's how I had my crash – worried sick about getting my icebreaker. I come on the job at eight in the morning, it's twelve o'clock noon, I still hadn't nailed a fare. I'm so upset I drive right through a furrier's window – into the beaver pelts, I wound up with the car radio in my stomach. And I mean *in* my stomach, too. I had folk music coming out of my asshole. So that was it.

TANDY   That was it?

OLDTIMER   That was it.

                 (MEREDITH *comes forth, humming a tune. Matter-of-
                 factly* SHE *drops the sheet, steps beneath the shower and
                 pulls the shower chain. Little cry of alarm when the water
                 hits her, but* SHE *enjoys it.* SHE *puts the sheet back on and
                 disappears in the haze.*)

TANDY   She come in here often?

OLDTIMER   Can't say. Nice set of maracas on her, though.

TANDY   Damn right.

OLDTIMER   You know, a lot of guys let the little old frankfurter rule
                 their heads. I always say, let your head rule the little old
                 frankfurter. You go along with that?

TANDY   (*After thinking it over.*)

                 Yeah! Well...

OLDTIMER   I never forget this rich bitch on Long Island had her eye
                 on me. I said, "Madame, that little old weenie you're so
                 interested in don't run the show. I'm the one that runs
                 the show." She didn't like that.

TANDY   (*Distracted.*)

                 That was unusual.

OLDTIMER   What's that?

ANDY   That girl. Taking a shower that way.

OLDTIMER   Nah, they got everything today. I got a son-in-law got
                 two toilets in one bathroom. He puts my two young
                 granddaughters on there, puts a tape recorder between

them and records what they say to each other while on the pot. That's my son-in-law's idea of a laugh.

TANDY   Is that right…

OLDTIMER   I knew I was going to have trouble with him.

(*The* TWO YOUNG MEN *come down and do a dancing and singing musical number from a popular Broadway musical comedy, complete with intricate steps, high kicks – in perfect unison.* THEY *have a little Panasonic-type player, of the cheap 42nd Street variety. This is the source of the music.* THEY *are quite good, semi-professional.* THEY *finish up big and then go back to their seats.*)

TANDY   This is some place.

OLDTIMER   Lucky they didn't slip on the pits.

(*Hoarse, guttural sound in the back, suspiciously from* BIEBERMAN's *direction.*)

OLDTIMER   What are you doing now?

BIEBERMAN   Gargling. I have a rough throat.

OLDTIMER   That's what I was afraid of. You watch your step, meathead.

(*To* TANDY.)

He starts blowing his nose, I'm going after him…

TANDY   They were very good – the dancers.

OLDTIMER   They do some good work. I never could enjoy a show much. I was always more interested in what was going on in the wings. I figured the real show, the good stuff, was going on back there. I'd rather sit and watch the wings than your top show on Broadway.

TANDY   I'd rather watch a show. I've never been that interested in the wings. But I see what you mean.

                 (MEREDITH *approaches*.)

MEREDITH   Are you all right?

TANDY   I'm fine. How was your shower?

MEREDITH   It was wonderful. Some day I'd like to meet the man who invented the needle-point showerhead and thank him for all the pleasure he's given me.

TANDY   Do you come here often?

MEREDITH   I don't know. All I can remember is that I was buying this little skirt at Paraphernalia…it couldn't have been this big and they were asking $17.50 for it –

BIEBERMAN   (*Appearing for the first time, on a ledge above* TANDY *and* MEREDITH. HE *speaks with a certain stopped-up anger.*)

                 You have no idea what those skirts have meant to members of my generation. What a skirt like that means to a fellow who could sit through the same movie seven times, willing to sell himself into bondage on a farm in Mississippi if he could see just an eighth of an inch of Ann Rutherford's inner thigh. And then there they are, out of the blue, those pitzi cocker skirts. And the girls wearing them, more beautiful than Ann Rutherford herself, are handing out massive looks at their thighs and crotches. No one has properly realized the effect of all that exposed and quivering flesh on the national character. And my generation is condemned to watch this country, representing one of the greatest social experiments in Western civilization, choke itself to death on an easy diet of tits and asses.

TANDY	Look, do you mind? We were having a private conversation...
BIEBERMAN	As you wish.
	(HE *drops his sheet, and, in his jockey shorts, begins to do a vigorous exercise squats, disgustingly close to* TANDY *and* MEREDITH.)
TANDY	Do you have to do that here?
OLDTIMER	He's just getting warmed up.
BIEBERMAN	It's just till I work up a good healthy sweat.
TANDY	Do it somewhere else, will you?
BIEBERMAN	(*Under his breath, as he moves off.*)
	Putz.
TANDY	(*Starting to chase* BIEBERMAN.)
	Hey!
	(*To* OLDTIMER.)
	He is disgusting. I never saw it until just now.
MEREDITH	You were a little hard on him.
TANDY	Was I? I didn't realize it. I was with the cops for a while. In the cultural section. I still have a little of the cop style left.
MEREDITH	Listen, if you were with the cops, could you tell me exactly where to kick someone so that's he's temporarily paralyzed and can't rape you – yet at the same time doesn't feel you're an insensitive person...?

TANDY	We stayed away from that stuff in the art department… What really puzzles me is that I am able to talk to you so easily.
MEREDITH	What do you mean?
TANDY	Well until recently, I had a great deal of trouble talking to yellow-haired girls. I felt I had to talk to them in verse or something…maybe wear special gloves. But apparently I've gotten over that.
MEREDITH	You're so nice. I love meeting a nice new person like you. But look, I don't want to get involved.
TANDY	Involved?
MEREDITH	I just can't go through with that again… I've had that this year…the phone calls… My skin… For what it does to my skin alone, it's not worth it… Look, I just don't have the strength for another affair… Maybe around Labour Day… If it's worth anything, it'll be good then, too… Will you call me then?
TANDY	(*Thinks awhile.*) I'll give you a ring.
MEREDITH	You're not angry, are you?
TANDY	I'm not angry.
MEREDITH	It's got nothing to do with you personally…you seem like a very sensual person.
OLDTIMER	There is a terrible stink in here. And I got a pretty good idea who's responsible for it.
BIEBERMAN	I haven't done a thing recently.

OLDTIMER	You'll never convince me of that. Whatever you're doing, cut it out – for my sake, for the sake of this steambath, and for the sake of America.
BIEBERMAN	I'm just sitting here, being natural, being myself...
OLDTIMER	That's what it is? Natural? ... That's what you've got to stop.
TANDY	(To MEREDITH.) Listen, what do you think of this place?
MEREDITH	I like it.
TANDY	Notice anything peculiar about it?
MEREDITH	It smells a little funny.
OLDTIMER	It sure as hell does.
BIEBERMAN	I haven't done a thing. I've been doing a crossword puzzle. (*To* TANDY.) What's a six-letter word that means little red spikes of corn?
OLDTIMER	How about "giggie"? Used in a sentence, it goes "Up your giggie."
BIEBERMAN	Lovely. (*Lights darken. A screen drops. Stock quotations flash across the screen as they do in a brokerage office. A fellow appears with a chair, sits down opposite the screen, and watches the quotations.*)
BROKER	(*Taking notes.*)

	They put that in for me.
TANDY	How's the market?
BROKER	Lousy – if you own good stocks. When I went into this business, I had one piece of advice for every one of my customers "Put your money in good stuff. Stay away from shit. That's what you want, find yourself another broker. I don't touch it." So what happens in the last five years? The good stuff lays there, shit goes right through the roof. Some of my customers, they went to other brokers, they bought shit, they made fortunes…
MEREDITH	(*Very trusting.*)
	Maybe the good stuff will improve – if it's really and truly good.
BROKER	Nah… It's too late for that…
	(*Screen disappears.* HE *picks up chair, recedes into the haze.*)
TANDY	That's the kind of thing I was talking about…
MEREDITH	What do you mean?
TANDY	A guy like that…in here…watching stocks…it's strange.
MEREDITH	I just wish the numbers wouldn't go by so fast. You hardly have any time to enjoy them. Am I wrong or have you been doing pretty well lately?
TANDY	I'm doing fine. I got a divorce. I quit the Police Academy. I'm writing a novel about Charlemagne. And I just got involved in a charity, helping brain-damaged welders. I was looking for a charity and that's the one I picked. They send out a terrific brochure. There are an

awful lot of them…welders…with brain damage…and they're really grateful when you help them. You should see the looks on some of those welders' faces. Could break your heart… I've been doing pretty well… I'm real close to my ten-year-old daughter.

MEREDITH   You have a ten-year-old daughter?

TANDY   Oh yeah, we just got back from Vegas.

MEREDITH   How did she like it?

TANDY   Well she thought little girls were allowed to gamble out there. She insisted that somewhere in Vegas there were slot machines that little girls were allowed to play. Well I read that you shouldn't disabuse a child of its fantasies, so I went along with the gag. So we spent four days looking for these special slot machines. Finally, when we got to the airport, I told her that little girls were allowed to play the airport slots just before they got on the plane. She said, "I told you, Daddy." We got very close on that trip. So I've been doing pretty well lately…

MEREDITH   Listen, you don't think…

TANDY   What? What?

MEREDITH   All I can remember is that Sheila and I were buying skirts at Paraphernalia. Then we went back to our high-rise apartment on 84th Street and, oh, yes, the Gristede's delivery boy was waiting behind the drapes, with a crazy look on his face, holding a blunt instrument…

TANDY   I was in my favourite restaurant, eating some Chinese food. I was just about to knock off a double order of Won Shih pancakes…

MEREDITH	You don't think?
TANDY	…We're dead? Is that what you were going to say? That's what I was going to say. That's what we are. The second I said it, I knew it. Bam! Dead! Just like that! Christ!
MEREDITH	I had it pictured an entirely different way.
TANDY	What's that?
MEREDITH	Being dead. I thought dying meant that you'd have to spend every day of your life at a different Holiday Inn. Then I decided it was seeing So Proudly We Hail with Veronica Lake over and over for the rest of time – in a place where there were no Mounds bars.
	(VOICE *is heard "Cold drinks, popcorn, Raisinettes, Goobers, and no Mounds bars".*)
TANDY	Don't pay any attention. Somebody's kidding around.
MEREDITH	(*With real loss.*)
	No Mounds bars…
TANDY	I don't know about you, but I'm not accepting this.
MEREDITH	What do you mean?
TANDY	I don't like the whole way it was done. Bam. Dead. Just like that. Just like you're a schmuck or something.
MEREDITH	What are you going to do?
TANDY	I'll do something. Don't worry. I'm a doer. If you had any idea of the agony I went through to change my life around you'd see why I'm so pissed off. To be picked off like this when I haven't even started to enjoy the good stuff.

MEREDITH	Well, how about me? I just had my first orgasm.
TANDY	Just now?
MEREDITH	No. While I was watching the David Frost Show. I was all alone, eating some Whip and Chill and I got this funny feeling.
TANDY	I'll tell you right now, I'm not going along with it. Not now. Not when I'm just getting off the ground. Another time, later on, they want me to be dead, fine. Not now. Uh-uh.
MEREDITH	I feel exactly the same way. How can I die? I haven't even bought any vinyl bust harnesses. And I've got to get my thighs down. Everything I eat has a little sign on it that says, "Do not pass, move directly to thighs." No, I absolutely can't die. Is there something you can do?
TANDY	I'll check around, see if I can find out something.
	(*Disappears in haze.*)
OLDTIMER	(*Reading newspaper.*)
	Says here they got a new gas, one gallon of it'll wipe out an entire enemy country…
BROKER	They got more than that. They got another one – just one drop in the water supply and the whole continent starts vomiting.
OLDTIMER	(*Sniffing.*)
	They could bottle the smell around here, they don't need any gas. You hear that back there?
BIEBERMAN	I'm not doing anything. I'm working on my toes.

OLDTIMER	I knew it, the son of a bitch. What are you doing to them?
BIEBERMAN	Trimming down the nails.
OLDTIMER	In here? This is where you picked? Cut it out will you, you slob, you're trying my patience.
TANDY	(*Taking aside* OLDTIMER.)
	Can I see you a second, Oldtimer?
OLDTIMER	What's on your mind, fella? Havin' trouble breathin'?
	(*Demonstrating.*)
	Suck it in through your mouth awhile.
TANDY	I was sitting over there with this girl…
OLDTIMER	(*Lasciviously.*)
	The one with them Chitty-Chitty Bang-Bangs?
TANDY	That's the one.
OLDTIMER	Don't let her get hold of your liverwurst. They get an arm-lock on that, they never let go.
TANDY	I got the idea that we were dead. And she agrees with me. Now I can take the dead part. That doesn't scare me. I get older, a little tired, fine. I even thought maybe later on, things go smoothly, maybe I'll knock myself off, make it simple. But the timing's all wrong now. I'm just getting off the ground. I'm in the middle of writing an historical novel – right in the fucking middle… I don't talk this way in the book… It's about Charlemagne. I've got a great new girlfriend– cooks me shish kebab. Bryn Mawr girl. And she still cooks shish kebab. Doesn't bother her a bit. And I never think about Wendy.

OLDTIMER	Wendy?
TANDY	My ex-wife. Wendy Tandy. Jesus, I just realized, she was Wendy Hilton, I turned her into Wendy Tandy. I probably blew the whole marriage right there. She never went for that name. Can't say that I blame her. Anyway, I don't think about her anymore. Weeks at a time. She could be out fucking the whole Royal Canadian Mounties, I don't give it a thought. I forgive her. She's a little weak. It's got nothing to do with me. So, you see, I'm really just starting a wonderful new chapter of my life. And along comes this death number – I thought maybe you could help me...
OLDTIMER	I hardly know what to say to you, fella. You come at me like a ten-foot wave.
TANDY	Is there a guy in charge? Somebody I can talk to? E. G. Marshall? Walter Pidgeon?
OLDTIMER	There's a guy comes around. I see him, I'll point him out.
TANDY	Thanks. You're not a bad skate. When we get out of this, maybe we can pal around together.
OLDTIMER	You probably smell the sea on me. Before I took up hackin' I worked the China coast for seventeen years. Me and my friend Ollie were the most widely respected duo west of Macao. We'd get ourselves a couple of juki-juki girls, take 'em up on deck and do a little missionary work with 'em anchored in front of Bruce Wong's Monkey Meat Shop in Hong Kong Harbour. They arrested Ollie for abusing himself into the holy water fountain at the Merchant Seaman's Chapel. He died in irons and I lost the best friend I ever had...

(*Fades off, a bit overcome with emotion.*)

MEREDITH   What did that old man say?

TANDY   He said there's a fellow around who seems to be in charge. That he'd point him out to me. Listen, how do you feel?

MEREDITH   I don't mind being nude, if that's what you mean. I just don't attribute that much importance to it.

TANDY   I know that. I can tell.

MEREDITH   I wouldn't want to get out there and do splits or anything.

TANDY   Who asked you to do splits? Is that what you think I want – splits?

MEREDITH   I just like to be nude sometimes. It's very tranquil.

TANDY   You see, that's where I really got a bum steer. The fellow who first taught me about sex – very smart guy, been all over, a Socialist – he told me, "Remember one thing, kid, women feel uncomfortable about being nude." So for a long time I went around covering up nude girls. They'd say, "What the hell are you doing?" and I'd say, "C'mon, I know you're uncomfortable." And I was wrong. I covered up some gorgeous women.

(*An* ATTENDANT *has been mopping up the steambath for awhile.* HE *comes clearly into view now.* HE *sings "Sorrento." Lah lah lah lah sentimento…lah lah lah lah sentirinco…lah lah lah lah ladimento…lah lah lah lah lah lah. Stops mopping to do the bridge, really performing now… lah lah lah lah lah lah…etc. After a big finish,* HE *says, "Thank you, music lovers" as though to a nightclub audience….*)

OLDTIMER	(*Signaling to* TANDY.)
	Psssst.
TANDY	(*Gesturing toward* ATTENDANT.)
	Him?
	(OLDTIMER *acknowledges correctness with a wink.*)
	You sure?
OLDTIMER	Yup...
TANDY	(*To* MEREDITH.)
	He says that's the fellow in charge.
MEREDITH	He's cute.
ATTENDANT	Hiya, baby.

(ATTENDANT *now wheels out what appears to be a console with a screen. It is a very tacky-looking affair. The screen is visible to the* ATTENDANT *but not to the audience. The console, from time to time, "answers" the* ATTENDANT *with little blipping noises as though taking note of his instructions. In between sections of his monologue, the Puerto Rican does little snatches of "Sorrento" again.*)

(*Leaning over console.*)

San Diego Freeway... All right, first thing, I want that Pontiac moving south past Hermosa Beach to crash into the light blue Eldorado coming the other way. Make it a head-on collision...the guy in the Chevy – his wife's got her ass out the window – it's the only way they get their kicks – they're going to jump the rail into the oncoming lane, and fuck up

a liquor salesman in a tan Cougar. No survivors...
All right, what's his name, Perez, the Puerto Rican
schmuck from the Bronx. The one who says, "My wife
and I – we are married forty years. We are born on the
same hill. There can be no trouble." He comes home
tonight, I want her screwing her brother. Perez walks
in, goes crazy, starts foaming at the mouth, the other
tenants in the building have to tie him to a radiator...
All right, the guy from St. Louis...bedspread
salesman...adopted all those Korean kids. Him, they
pick up in the men's room of the Greyhound Bus
Terminal, grabbing some truckdriver's schvontz.
They ask around, find out he's been doing it for
years... The kids get shipped back to Korea.
Now, here's one I like... The screenwriter flying out
to Beverly Hills. Coming on with the broads. Here's
what happens. Over Denver, a stewardess throws
a dart in his eye. No doctor on board. He was to
go all the way to Los Angeles like that. Pheww...!
The hooker – little fat one – been peddling her ass
in Barcelona for three years – took on 4,000 sailors
– she's saved up a few bucks, she's gonna go straight.
Get ready. This is rough. I want her found in a dirt pit
on Montauk Highway. And if her parents really carry
on, I mean really piss and moan, then go after the
sister, too, the homely one. Give her an ear infection.
Now, the producer up in New Haven. Never had a hit.
Doing a $750,000 musical...the whole show depends
on the female star. All right a police dog gets loose
in the theatre and bites her tits off. The understudy
is scared as shit, but she goes on anyway. Bombsville.
Next day, the guy gets out of the business...

(*Starts to leave, returns.*)

Wait a minute. I got an idea. Back to the Freeway. That guy whose radiator boiled over...on the side of the road, saw the whole thing. Thought he got away clean. He gets knocked unconscious by the bare-assed broad. Never knew what hit him. That's all for now.

(HE *picks up mop and continues to work on the steambath floor.* HE *sings "Sorrento." And* HE *disappears for the moment in the haze.*)

TANDY   You sure that's the fellow in charge?

OLDTIMER   That's him all right. He runs the show.

TANDY   What's his name?

OLDTIMER   Morty.

TANDY   A Puerto Rican guy? Morty?

OLDTIMER   It's Spanish.

                   (*Pronouncing name with Spanish inflection.*)

                   Mawwrrr-teee.

TANDY   (*To* MEREDITH.)

                   He's sure that's the fellow in charge.

MEREDITH   Well if he isn't, he certainly has a rich imagination.

TANDY   You say he hangs around here.

OLDTIMER   All the time. He comes and goes.

                   (ATTENDANT *returns, singing softly, sweeping, goes to console again. His voice is much softer now.*)

ATTENDANT   Okay, the other side of the coin. The kid in a hospital in Trenton, beautiful kid, works for Carvel's. Got his foot shot off in a stick-up. The night nurse comes in, jerks him off under the covers. Lovely broad, little old, but she really knows what she's doing... Give Canada a little more rain...

That Indian tribe outside of Caracas. Sick little guys, they ain't got a hundred bucks between 'em... Government doesn't give a shit. CBS moves in, shoots a jungle series there, throws a lot of money around...

The old lady with the parakeet, flies out the window, flies back in...

Wellesley girl, parents got a lot of dough, she's sitting on a ledge – 35th floor of the Edison Hotel. A cop crawls out after her, tells her she's a pain in the ass. They go back in, watch a hockey game on TV... And clean up that garbage in the lobby... It's disgusting... That spade they beat up at Chicago Police headquarters. Got a landing strip for a head. All right, kill the cop who roughed him up – and then send the spade over to Copenhagen for a vacation. At least three months. I don't know who picks up the tab. He's got a cousin in the music business. Records for Decca... All right, that's enough good stuff.

VOICE	You need one more.
ATTENDANT	Christ, I'm exhausted. Uhh... Put bigger bath towels in all the rooms at the Tel Aviv Hilton Hotel.
VOICE	Terrific!
ATTEDANT	You kidding, buddy...?
	(*Exits.*)
MEREDITH	I liked him much more the second time.

TANDY	He's got some style. Who's he think he is?
OLDTIMER	God.
TANDY	You believe that?
OLDTIMER	I'm not saying yes and I'm not saying no. I been around and I seen a lot of strange things in my time. I once stood in an Algerian pissoir urinal and watched the head of a good friend of mine come rolling up against my size 12 moccasins like a bowling ball. Cut right off at the neck. He's gotten into a little scuffle with some Gurkhas. May have called one of them a fag. Didn't know there aren't any fag Gurkhas.
TWO YOUNG MEN	That's what you think.
TANDY	Well what the hell are we supposed to do, just stay here?
BROKER	There's nothing that great out there. The market stinks. You don't make a quarter unless you're in pork bellies. That ain't investing.
TANDY	I'm not going along with this. For Christ's sakes, I'm in the middle of writing an historical novel. About Charlemagne. I got all that research to do. So far I've been going on instinct. What the hell do I know about Charlemagne? But the book feels good...
MEREDITH	And I've got an appointment at the beauty parlour. To get a Joan of Arc haircut. And my roommate Sheila and I are going to make little plastic surrealistic doodads and sell them to boutiques.
TANDY	I'll get us out of this. Did you try the door?
MEREDITH	No, why?

TANDY	Don't try it. I'm pretty sure it doesn't open. If I find out for sure, I'll get claustrophobia… Is there another way out? What's this door? (*Referring to second door at opposite side of the stage.*)
OLDTIMER	You go through there.
TANDY	When's that?
OLDTIMER	Hard to say… We had a guy, a baker, he put him in there.
TANDY	What did he do?
OLDTIMER	Not much. Beat the Puerto Rican in arm-wrestling.
BROKER	Had a little trouble with his baking though. Everything used to burn up on him. Pastries, cupcakes…meat pies…
TANDY	Don't tell me about cupcakes now…no cupcakes. When he puts you in there, does he let you out? (OLDTIMER *chuckles, as if to say, "Are you kidding?".*) And that's it, the two doors?
OLDTIMER	That's it. That's the whole cheesecake. (TANDY *very casually sidles up to entrance door, tries it. It doesn't open. Tries a little harder, still won't.*)
TANDY	About the way I figured. I'll get us out of here, don't worry. You with me?
MEREDITH	Are you serious? Of course. But you haven't said how.
TANDY	I'll get us out. You'll find I do most things well. Of course, I have never been able to get out to Kennedy Airport. On my own. I can get near it, but never really

in it. The Van Wyck Expressway scene really throws me.

MEREDITH   You're sort of inconsistent, aren't you?

TANDY   You noticed that, eh? I admit it. I've got wonderful qualities, but getting out to airports is not one of them. Don't worry, though, I'll get us out of here. By sheer strength of will and determination. I believe I can do anything if I really put my mind to it. I've always felt that even if I had a fatal illness, with an army of diseased phagocytes coursing through my body in triumph, if I really decided to, I could reverse the course of those phagocytes and push them the hell back where they belong...

MEREDITH   The world admires that kind of determination.

TANDY   You're damned right.

MEREDITH   What if we really are dead, though?

TANDY   I know. I've been trying not to think about it. No more toast. No more clams. Clams oregano.

MEREDITH   No more playing with Mr. Skeffington.

TANDY   Mr. Skeffington? Wait a minute, don't tell me. That's your cat.

MEREDITH   Yes.

TANDY   How can you compare that in seriousness to the things I'm talking about? I'm talking about big stuff. No more sneezing. No more being under the covers. No more airline stewardesses...Newsweek...Jesus, no more Newsweek. Wait a minute, I'll get this straightened out right now...

(HE *approaches* ATTENDANT, *who has come mopping into view.*)

Say, fella…

ATTENDANT   You addressing I?

TANDY   That's right. What's the deal around here? The Oldtimer says you're God.

ATTENDANT   Some people call me that.

TANDY   But that's ridiculous… a Puerto Rican…

ATTENDANT   The Puerto Ricans go back hundreds of years. Millions. There were Puerto Ricans in Greece, Rome. Diogenes – very big, very strong Puerto Rican. Too many people make fun of the Puerto Ricans. Very fine people. Lots of class. We got Josй Torres, Mario Procaccino…

TANDY   All right, I'll go along with you for a second. You're God. Why would you be sweeping up, a lowly job like that?

ATTENDANT   It's therapeutic. I like it. It's easy on the nerves.

TANDY   God… A Puerto Rican steambath attendant. That'll be day.

ATTENDANT   Look, I'll tell you what, fella. You say I'm not God. All right. You got it. I'm not God. Fabulous. You got what you want.

(*Pointing to* BIEBERMAN.)

He's God.

OLDTIMER   He ain't God. He's a slob.

BIEBERMAN	Everything doesn't pay off in cleanliness. There are other virtues.
OLDTIMER	You stink to the high heavens.
TWO YOUNG MEN	We've reached the conclusion that you're being much too tough on him.
OLDTIMER	Don't you two ever split up?
TWO YOUNG MEN	(*Seductively.*) Make us an offer.
ATTENDANT	Mister, just don't bug me. All right? I got a lot on my mind.
TANDY	There's another one. God talking slang. How can I go along with that?
ATTENDANT	I talk any way I want, man. The Lord speaks in funny ways. Remember that. You want to discuss the relatively of mass, the Lorentz Transformation, galactic intelligence, I'll give you that too. Just don't bug me. All right? Don't be no wise ass.
TANDY	That was more like it. You had me going there for a second. I respect anyone who really knows something, my work being as transitory as it is. It's when you talk dirty...
ATTENDANT	The way I talk, the way I talk... Don't you see that's just a little blink of an eye in terms of the universe, the job I got to do? The diameter of an electron is one ten-trillionth of an inch. And you're telling me I shouldn't talk dirty. Let me talk the way I want. Let me relax a little.
TANDY	I can't see it. You're not God.

ATTENDANT   You can't see it? Don't see it. I got things to do.

                 (*Approaches console screen again.*)

                 All right, give that girl on the bus a run on her body
                 stocking. I want to close up that branch of Schrafft's...
                 And   send   up   a   bacon-and-lettuce-and-tomato
                 sandwich, hold the mayo. You burn the toast, I'll smite
                 you down with my terrible swift sword.

                 (*Leaves the console.*)

TANDY   I still don't buy it. That could be an ordinary TV screen.
                 You could have been watching *Laugh*-In.

ATTENDANT   Laugh-In?

                 (*Goes over to console.*)

                 Cancel Laugh-In. You still want to fool around?

TANDY   I don't watch Laugh-In. Only thing I watch on TV is
                 pro football. Gets better every year. Look, you're asking
                 me to buy a whole helluva lot. You're challenging every
                 one of my beliefs.

ATTENDANT   You think I care about your beliefs? With the job I got
                 on my mind?

TANDY   You care. I may be one man, but there exists within me
                 the seed of all mankind.

ATTENDANT   Very good. I'm going to give you a ninety on that.

TANDY   I used to tell that to my art-appreciation students over
                 at the Police Academy.

ATTENDANT   Nice bunch of boys.

TANDY You mean to tell me that you control every action on earth by means of that monitor over there? Every sneeze, every headache, every time a guy cuts himself? How can you possibly do so much?

ATTENDANT I go very fast. You got to move like crazy. You can't stop and talk to every schmuck who comes along...

(GOTTLIEB *comes in with a tray.*)

GOTTLIEB Your BLT down, sir.

ATTENDANT Thank you. What do I owe you for that?

GOTTLIEB Are you kidding, sire?

ATTENDANT Just thought I'd ask. You don't have to get snotty about it.

(GOTTLIEB *goes off.* ATTENDANT *eats.*)

TANDY I don't know. It's awfully hard to accept. I've heard of having your faith tested, but this is ridiculous

ATTENDANT (*Chewing BLT.*)

And who said you could speak while I was eating?

TANDY All right. I'm sorry. I beg your pardon. One minute you're casual, the next you're formal. How can I keep up with you?

ATTENDANT Changeable, mysterious, infinite, unfathomable. That's my style...

TANDY Yeah – except that you're not God.

ATTENDANT That's the conclusion you reached after all the time I spent with you? I'll tell you right now you're getting me roped off. I get roped off, watch out. Then you're really in trouble.

(*Pulling himself together.*)

All right. I'll tell you what. You say I'm not God, right?

TANDY   Right.

ATTENDANT   (*Pulling out deck of cards, and spreading them, like a fan.*)

All right. Pick a card, any card.

TANDY   What's that gonna prove?

ATTENDANT   Go ahead, just do what I'm tellin' you. You'll see.

(TANDY *picks card.*)

You look at it?

TANDY   Yes.

ATTENDANT   (*Squinting eyes.*)

Okay...you got the...King of Hearts... Right?

(BROKER, *most nervous of all characters, applauds.*)

TANDY   All right. You did it. So what?

ATTENDANT   So there y'are.

TANDY   There I am what? You do a simple card trick that any kid can do – a retarded kid can do – and I'm supposed to think you're God.

ATTENDANT   Can you do it?

TANDY   No, I can't do it. I can't even deal a hand of blackjack. But there are hundreds of guys who can do that trick.

In every village and hamlet in the country. What the hell does that prove?

ATTENDANT   Not in the hamlets. It's not that easy. In the villages, maybe, but not in the hamlets. All right, I show you a trick that's not as easy as it seems, you won't buy it. Fair enough. You're pushing me to the wall. I'm not saying a word. Now, check my pants. And easy on the corporeal contact.

(TANDY *begrudgingly does so.*)

Anything in there?

TANDY   There's nothing in there.

ATTENDANT   (*With a flourish.*)

Now…

(*Pulls out a long multi-coloured scarf.*) How's that?

(*Drapes it over* MEREDITH *as a shawl.*)

TANDY   I've seen it about a dozen times.

ATTENDANT   Where?

TANDY   On the Sullivan Show. These Slavic guys come over here and do that trick. On a bicycle. Someone tells them they can come here and clean up. Sullivan's the only one who'll give them a break. They make a few bucks, you never hear from them again. They go right back to those Slavic countries. Look, I'm sorry. I don't know quite how to say this, but you are not even putting a dent in me. What kind of second-rate horse-shit is this?

ATTENDANT   (*Gesturing as though he is pulling a knife out of his chest.*)

Madre de Dios. You hurt my feelings just now. You know that, don't you?

TANDY

There's a perfect example. God with his feelings hurt. Ridiculous.

ATTENDANT

My feelings are not supposed to get hurt? Once in a while? All right. Now I'm really going to give you one.

(*Calling into the wings.*)

Gottlieb.

(ASSISTANT *runs out with a footlocker kept shut by a huge padlock. Sets it down.*)

Thanks, Gottlieb, I won't forget this.

(*To* TANDY.)

All right. Check the lock.

TANDY

(*Following instructions.*)

I checked it.

ATTENDANT

Is it strong?

TANDY

Very strong, very powerful. Big deal.

ATTENDANT

All right. Observez-vous.

(GOTTLIEB *ties his hands behind him.* HE *kneels down and, with his teeth, sawing away like a bulldog, chews and chews and finally springs the lock.* GOTTLIEB *has been doing an accompanying song-and-dance routine, neatly timed, as though they have been through this many times before. With lock in his teeth, arms upraised, like a trapeze man,* ATTENDANT *acknowledges applause.* GOTTLIEB *throws a few ribbons of confetti over his head.*)

Voila!

TANDY

It was okay, I admit. It was a little better than the others. At least you're showing me a little something. Look, I don't know how to get this across to you, but you are not reaching me with this stuff. Maybe I'm crazy.

(*To* STEAMBATH PEOPLE, *who are visible through the haze now.*)

Are you people impressed?

OLDTIMER

Only one fella I know could do that, fella named Radio. Sneaky little bugger, ran into him in New Guinea. Used to go crazy over radios. If you were carrying one, he'd figure out a way to get it away from you. Old Radio could have picked that lock with his teeth, no question about it...

ATTENDANT

There y'are. You heard what the man said. Only one other fellow could've pulled off that stunt — Radio.

TANDY

Wonderful. Look, I can't help it. Sue me. I'm not moved. If you had made one interesting intellectual assault on my mind, maybe that would do it.

ATTENDANT

De gustibus non est disputandum.

TANDY

That's it? That's the intellectual assault? Freshman English?

ATTENDANT

Have you ever really pondered it? Savoured it? Rolled it around on your tongue and really tasted of its fruit?

TANDY

That's right, I have. And it's nothing. It's garbage. It's not the kind of insight to make the senses reel.

ATTENDANT

(*Gathering others about him.*)

Consider the mind, an independent substance implanted within the soul and incapable of being destroyed... The City of Satan, whatever its artifices in art, war, or philosophy, was essentially corrupt and impious, its joy but a comic mask and its beauty the whitening of a sepulchre. It stood condemned before man's better conscience by its vanity, cruelty, and secret misery, by its ignorance of all that it truly behooved a man to know who was destined to immortality... Or how about this one: "A little philosophy inclineth man's mind to atheism, but depth in philosophy bringeth men's minds about to religion."

TANDY

Much better. Maybe I could even chew on some of that. But you still haven't got me. All I can see is a fairly interesting guy – for a Puerto Rican. If I ran into you at a bar – a Puerto Rican bar – maybe we could kick around a few ideas. All I'm saying is I don't see God yet. Where's God?

ATTENDANT

You don't see God, huh? Boy, you're some pistol. All right, here comes a little number that is going to make your head swim. You happen to be in luck, fella, because you caught me at cocktail time and I'm dry as a bone. Gottlieb... Now you watch this carefully...

(GOTTLIEB *emerges with tray of drinks.*)

How many drinks you estimate are on that tray?

TANDY

Ten...

(ATTENDANT *begins to knock them off, one at a time.*)

...and you don't even have to bother drinking them, because I can name you two lushes out there on Eighth Avenue who can do the same thing... I mean, what is this... it's not even as good as the trunk. You might have snapped off a few teeth on that one...but this cheap, trivial, broken-down, ninth-rate...

(*As* HE *speaks,* GOTTLIEB *returns, struggling to bring in an enormous whiskey sour, one that towers above* TANDY'*s head.* TANDY *is thunderstruck.*)

Are you mad?

ATTENDANT   Un momento?

(HE *leaps to top tier of column, sits opposite rim of glass, pulls out a straw and takes a sip.*)

Delicious. That son of a bitch makes some drink.

(ATTENDANT *finishes up with a flourish, leaps down.*)

All right, what have you got to say to that, baby? Incidentally, you like the cherry – go ahead, don't be embarrassed...

TANDY   It was pretty good. All right. I take that back. Fair is fair. It was great. My hat goes off to you. It was really remarkable. I figure the odds were about fifty to one against. I hardly know how to say this next thing, but I'm still not buying it. The God routine.

ATTENDANT   You're still not buying it?

TANDY   No sir. The fact that I just said "sir" will give you an indication that I'm really impressed. You got a lot going for you. But I'm not really there yet. If I said I bought the whole thing, you'd know I wasn't being straight. It would be an injustice of a kind. A real sell-out.

ATTENDANT   So then you still don't buy it.

TANDY

No sir.

ATTENDANT

You really making me work, boy. All right. I have but one choice, my son.

(*Gestures.*)

Shazam…

(*Stage, theatre, suddenly fill with deafening organ music, churchlike, ancient, soaring, almost unbearable. Theatre then fills with angels or other miraculous and heavenly effects.* ATTENDANT *stands majestically, his head crowned with celestial light.* HE *ascends to highest tier in steambath. Music is deafening in its churchlike call to the divinity. Voice of* ATTENDANT, *magnified a hundredfold, similar to that of Cecil B. DeMille, booms out.*)

ATTENDANT'S
VOICE

ASCRIBE UNTO THE LORD YE KINDREDS OF THE PEOPLES…
ASCRIBE UNTO THE LORD
GLORY AND STRENGTH…
ASCRIBE UNTO THE LORD
THE GLORY DUE UNTO HIS NAME
BRING AN OFFERING
AND COME UNTO HIS COURTS
OH, WORSHIP THE LORD
IN THE BEAUTY OF HOLINESS
TREMBLE BEFORE HIM
ALL THE EARTH…

(*One by one, the* STEAMBATH PEOPLE *drop to their knees.* TANDY *looks around, observes that* HE *is the only one standing.* HE *shrugs, goes to one knee.*)

CURTAIN

ACT II

(PEOPLE *are all lying around, exhausted, as though after a heavy night-long bacchanal.*)

(BROKER *comes skipping in with a rope.*)

BROKER   (*To* TANDY.)

You ought to try this… Really gets the weight off you… Look in the mirror sometime while you're doing it. Everything moves. The stuff way inside – where you have the real weight – that's moving too…

(*Stops jumping.*)

How much do you weigh…?

TANDY   Me? Around 190…195…somewhere in there…

BROKER   I'm 179 myself. I'd like to lose around ten, twelve pounds. Twelve pounds, I'd feel like a tiger…

(*Grabbing some flesh around his waist.*)

I got to lose it around here – that's where it's rough… 'specially when you get around my age…

TANDY   That's right…

BROKER   One hundred sixty-eight. That's my perfect weight. You should see me at 168. Never seen anything like it…

TANDY	I bet you look great…
BROKER	I do. I get up in the middle, high seventies, forget it. It's all gone… You want to hear something else…?
TANDY	Shoot.
BROKER	When I'm 168, I get a beautiful bowel movement… How about you? You pretty regular?
TANDY	I don't want to hurt your feelings or anything, but I'm really not that interested in your bowel movements…
BROKER	I can see that… Sorry if I was presumptuous…
TANDY	Perfectly All right…
BROKER	I once bought a stock at 168 – my exact weight… Fellow who recommended it said this is a stock you don't worry about. It goes off, for argument's sake, ten, twenty, fifty points, I don't care if it goes off a hundred points…you don't worry about this stock. So I hold it. And it does go off ten, twenty, over a hundred points. The stock is now selling at a fast ten points. So I call the guy. It's down to ten, I say. When do I start worrying? "Never," he says. He just wasn't a worrier. I lost every penny… Shows you…go trust people… I should've stuck to ferns…
TANDY	Ferns?
BROKER	That's right. I was in the fern game for a while. A lot of people go in for ferns, you'd be surprised. I was cleaning up. But I couldn't take the social pressure… Guy at a party'd ask me what do you do, I'd say I'm in ferns… How do you think that made me feel?
OLDTIMER	Turn off that TV set…

BROKER	I had to get out…
BIEBERMAN	I'm watching a wonderful forties' movie. And it's down very low.
OLDTIMER	Turn it off, I tell you. I'm trying to catch a quick snooze. Turn it off or I'll come up there and kick you in the bazanzas…
BIEBERMAN	What are they?
OLDTIMER	Never mind. You'll find out fast enough if I kick you there.
BIEBERMAN	Anti-Semite.
OLDTIMER	I'm an anti-stinkite. That's what you got to worry about. Now turn it off, I tell you…
BIEBERMAN	(*Always a little bitter, angry when* HE *speaks, spitting the words out deliberately.*)

BIEBERMAN

I suppose it never occurred to you that every smile, every whisper, every puff of a cigarette taken by my generation was inspired by the forties' movie. That my generation wouldn't know how to mix a drink, drive a car, kiss a girl, straighten a tie – if it weren't for Linda Darnell and George Brent… That the sole reason for my generation's awkward foundering in the darkness is that Zachary Scott is gone…and I assure you that Dennis Hopper is no substitute…

OLDTIMER

I'll tell you what your generation needs — a movie that instructs you on how to smell like a human being. You can star in it.

(*To* TANDY.)

How can he even see the screen with all this steam…

| BIEBERMAN | When it gets too dense, I smear it off with a corner of my jockey shorts. |

| OLDTIMER | I spent four years in the Philippines I never ran into a slob like that. |

| | (*Suddenly clutches at his chest, as though having a heart attack, then realizes this is impossible and gestures as if to say "The hell with it".*) |

| TANDY | C'mon, you guys, knock it off. You're supposed to be dead. Act like it. |

| MEREDITH | It's wonderful the way they listen to you. |

| TANDY | It's probably that time I spent with the cops. It really changes you. Even when you're in the art department. One day they invited me on an assault case and these two detectives, kidding around, threw me out on a fire escape with this huge transvestite – had arms like a boilermaker. Anyway, we're on the thirty-fifth floor, we start grappling with each other, and I figure it's either me or it. So I bit him in the ear. Well, it must have turned him on because all of a sudden he confesses that he electrocuted a hippy in Vermont. Well, I told him I was kidding around, I wasn't a real dick, but he just kept confessing and I kept biting and finally they hauled us both back through the window and booked him on the Vermont thing and me on a morals charge – I'm just kidding... I finally had to get out of the cops, it was a terrible place...there was one thing – I could always run up a tab at the Automat... |

| MEREDITH | Oh, my God... |

| TANDY | What's wrong? |

MEREDITH   I just remembered. I haven't paid my Bloomingdale's bill.

TANDY   When was it due?

MEREDITH   Last Monday…now they'll probably send me one of those thin gray envelopes… You have no idea how much I hate those envelopes…

TANDY   But it's ridiculous. You can't pay your bills now. The store will understand.

MEREDITH   Bloomingdale's! I don't know why they insist on making you feel so terrible. Any other store – Saks, Bendel's – if you don't pay your bill they assume you're in Acapulco. Not Bloomingdale's. Right for the throat. "In ten days if you have not paid your bill, we are cutting off your charge account and telling your parents, friends, and the principal of the first school you attended…"

TANDY   Look, obviously none of this has sunk in. We're in big trouble. We could be stuck in this lousy steambath forever. You're sitting around talking Bloomingdale's. You saw that Puerto Rican guy… He wasn't kidding around…

MEREDITH   That was fun.

TANDY   What do you mean?

MEREDITH   The part where we got down on our knees. We used to do that at Marymount every morning, first thing, and it was freezing. It was fun getting down on a nice warm floor for a change…

TANDY   It wasn't any fun for me. I got to get out of here. I got all this Charlemagne research to do. There's going to be a whole Charlemagne revival, I can tell. Books, movies, musical comedies. Dolls – that's right. Little Charlemagne dolls. And I'll be left out of it. Where is that guy? I'm going to take another shot at him.

(*Disappears for a moment in the haze.*)

BIEBERMAN   Anyone have some pimple lotion...

OLDTIMER   There he goes again, the cocksucker...

BIEBERMAN   Well, I can't control my complexion, can I?

OLDTIMER   Of course you can. Ever hear of cutting down on malteds?

BIEBERMAN   I'll never cut down on malteds, never.

OLDTIMER   Well, then, don't come to me with your pimples, you stupid bastard.

BIEBERMAN   Malteds are the marijuana of my generation.

OLDTIMER   Your generation...what the hell generation is that?

BIEBERMAN   It went by very quickly... It was Dolf Camilli, Dane Clark, Uncle Don, Ducky Medwick and out...

OLDTIMER   Sounds like a real bunch of winners.

BIEBERMAN   We produced Norman Podhoretz.

OLDTIMER   Congratulations...

(*To the* BROKER.)

Who the fuck is Norman Podhoretz?

BROKER   Probably some wealthy bastard who made it when you could keep it.

TANDY   (*Entering.*)

We're all set.

MEREDITH	What's up?
TANDY	I've got a whole bunch of carpet tacks.
MEREDITH	Wow. Where did you get them?
TANDY	They got an old carpet rolled up back there.
MEREDITH	What good'll they do?
TANDY	Plenty. Don't undersell them. I once saw a guy with only a handful of carpet tacks get the best of two armed cops.
MEREDITH	That's remarkable, overpowering two policemen that way.
TANDY	That's right. Where is that guy? Listen, we get out, I'd like you to see my apartment. I've got big steel bars on the windows – I had a few robberies – but I've got the bars painted in psychedelic colors. I've got huge double security locks – they're painted in psychedelic colors too. Burglar alarm – same deal.
MEREDITH	I'd love to see your apartment.
TANDY	I'd like you to see it. It's not a horny thing. I won't jump on you or anything.
MEREDITH	Oh, I know that…
TANDY	Well, as a matter of fact, it is a partially horny thing. You're a very good-looking girl…but I'm also proud of the apartment.
MEREDITH	Don't you have a girlfriend?

TANDY	Oh yes, I've got an ex-wife, a mistress, a mother…I'm covered on all sides. Now I just need a girl…
MEREDITH	I understand. You just want someone totally uncomplicated.
TANDY	That's right.
MEREDITH	It's only fair to tell you that I can only sleep with one man at a time. If I slept with you I might reach across in the middle of the night and think I was stroking Raymondo…
TANDY	Raymondo? Listen, don't worry about it. I just want you to see my place sometime… Listen, you and your roommate don't…I mean…together.
MEREDITH	Make scenes?… Oh no…we don't do that.
TANDY	I hope you don't take offense… I was just checking.
MEREDITH	We don't anymore, that is. We did take a mascaline trip recently with one of my stockbroker friends. It didn't work out. It turned into a sort of business trip.
TANDY	Well, look, I don't need that right now. I got my hands full the way it is… It's just that when you work with the cops you see a lot of crazy things, you get ideas. You should go out on a few homicides. You should see what incensed Mexicans do to their common-law wives when they step out of line. Believe me, you'd never want to be a Mexican common-law wife.
MEREDITH	Oh, I don't know. I hear Cuernavaca's beautiful.
OLDTIMER	(*To* BROKER.)
	Toughest son of a bitch I ever knew used to dress up like Carmen Miranda. They found him floating five

kilometres outside Hamburg Harbour...all those bananas bobbing in the water.

(ATTENDANT *enters,* GOTTLIEB *along with him.*)

ATTENDANT   All right, everybody, campfire time. Gottlieb, give out the Mounds bars.

(GOTTLIEB *distributes candy bars to* STEAMBATH INHABITANTS, *who gather round an improvised campfire site.*)

MEREDITH   (*Accepting a candy bar.*)

Oh, I love these...

TANDY   (*Calling* ATTENDANT *aside.*)

Listen, I want to talk to you about getting out of here. I got a lot of deals going on the outside, a lot of things to clear up. I don't know if you know anything about Charlemagne...

ATTENDANT   The Puerto Rican?

TANDY   Cute. Listen, I haven't mentioned it yet, but I want you to know that was very impressive stuff you did, drinking all the stuff, those lights...very good...

ATTENDANT   I saw you on your knees.

TANDY   One knee. I just went down on one knee... Maybe that's half-assed, I don't know. Maybe a straight solid guy – a Henry Cabot Lodge – would have either given you both knees or said the hell with it...I don't know. I figured you run the place I'll throw you one knee. A little respect. Meanwhile, I got to talk to you about getting out of here. I don't belong here, I don't need this.

ATTENDANT	You know what I don't need? Right now? Aggravation.
TANDY	God, aggravated. There's another hot one.
ATTENDANT	Listen, if you're God, the name of the game is aggravation. Anyway, I don't want to hear anymore. You say another word, baby, I'll become wrathful and vengeance-seeking.

(*Gestures to* BROKER *to begin.*)

BROKER	For twenty years I was mad at my partner.
ATTENDANT	Once upon a time…
BROKER	Excuse me… Once upon a time for twenty years I was mad at my partner.
ATTENDANT	Hold it a second. Any broads in this story?
BROKER	No.
ATTENDANT	Gottlieb, you want to stay?

(GOTTLIEB *shrugs.*)

He likes serious stuff, too, otherwise I wouldn't keep him around. But once in a while he likes to hear about broads. Go ahead…

BROKER	We were partners for twenty years. Somehow he had everything – a glass house, schnauzer dogs, cuff links you should have seen the size of them… And I'm living in three rooms in Washington Heights. It was eating at me. I figure we're partners. How come I don't have a glass house and schnauzer dogs? So one day I went to visit him in his house and I put it to him. He listens to my complaints, goes inside, and comes out with a cheque for eight hundred dollars. Well, I couldn't figure

out that cheque. How did he come up with that figure? But amazingly, I wasn't angry. After all, eight hundred was eight hundred. So I went outside and sat on the golf course. I never liked to play, but I do like to sit on a golf course. And that's how they found me, sitting on a director's chair, right near the fourth hole, with the eight-hundred-dollar cheque in my lap and my head thrown back like this.

(HE *demonstrates, throwing back his head, opening his mouth wide and baring his teeth grotesquely.*)

They all came back and when they saw me, they all made that face too, that same face. They all threw back their heads and opened their mouths and made the same dead face I had.

(HE *demonstrates again.*)

ATTENDANT   It's going to be hard to give you a ninety on that one.

MEREDITH   I thought it was fascinating. I wonder why they wanted to make that face.

(SHE *tries it.*)

OLDTIMER   That's easy. They wanted to taste a little death without really being dead.

MEREDITH   Oh, I see. Gee, this is good. It's just like Camp Aurora. Who's next?

TWO YOUNG MEN   We both hung ourselves for love of the same boy—a swing dancer in the national company of Zorba. We never realized we could love someone that... indifferent...we loved the way he moved...the rough carving of his arms...the way the veins were printed on them. We'd go to the all-night skating rinks... And then, unaccountably, he simply left the show – and went back to school in North Carolina. Totally unmarked by us—as though we'd been a slight change in the direction of the wind. Neither of us meant a thing to him...We were no more than a pair of cats that crossed his path in a strange village and slowed his walk for a moment. He was beautiful.

ATTENDANT   Tell you the truth, I never went in very much for fag stories.

MEREDITH   I thought it was very touching.

ATTENDANT   I'm a sympathizer...but they don't really satisfy me.

TWO YOUNG MEN   Well, you wrote it.

ATTENDANT   That's true. But you know how it is when you're a writer. You write some stuff you don't like. Who's got a good one?

TANDY   This is very unjust. You've obviously set this thing up for your own amusement.

ATTENDANT   And you don't like that. I'm not allowed to have a few laughs. Listen, you been giving me a hard time ever since you come in here... You show up...you don't like it...you hand me this Charlemagne routine... I'm going to do a bad thing to you now.

TANDY   (*Alarmed.*)

               What's that? I admit I'm frightened. What are you going to do?

               (*Looks at second door.*)

               You're not going to put me in there, are you?

ATTENDANT

No.

(*Points to* OLDTIMER.)

I'm putting him in there.

(*To* TANDY.)

You come in here…you're looking for fair, reasonable…
Where'd you get that from? Old man…

OLDTIMER

(*Rising.*)

My time, eh?

ATTENDANT

That's right, baby.

OLDTIMER

Well, that's okay. I done everything. I once had a pair of
perfectly matched wooden-legged frauleins powder me
up from head to toe and dress me up in silk drawers.
I run up against a Greek sailor walking around for
thirty years with a lump on his chest he took to be a
natural growth. Turned out to be the unborn fetus of a
twin brother he'd spent all his life hankering for. I seen
most everything. I dipped my beak in Madrid, Spain;
Calcutta, India; Leningrad, Russia, and I never once
worried about them poisoning the water. I had myself
the fifth-richest woman in Sydney, Australia, genuine
duchess she was, all dressed up in a tiger suit; by the
time I finished with her I had them stripes going the
wrong way. I played a pretty good trumpet. I had to
face the fact that I was no Harry James, but then again,
Sir Harry couldn't go in there and break up a Polish
wedding the way I could. I talked back to the biggest
guys. Didn't bother me. I didn't care if it was me way
down in the valley, hollering up at Mount Zion. I'd
holler up some terrific retorts. You're not going to show
me anything I haven't seen. I paid my dues.

(*Starts to go.*)

And I'll tell you something else: if anything in there kicks me, you watch and see if I don't bite.

(HE *hitches himself up with great dignity and does a sailor's dance, then a proud old-man's walk into the grated room.*)

ATTENDANT   Old man had a lot of balls.

TANDY   Damn right.

(*To* ATTENDANT.)

Listen, I was the wise guy. Why didn't you send me in there?

ATTENDANT   That's direct. I don't work that way. I always put a little spin on the ball. Okay. This is the last one. I want live actors this time.

(*A cheap lower-class bar is set up – or at least the skeletal representation of one.* TWO MEN *stand on opposite sides of the bar. One is a* LONGSHOREMAN; *the other is* GOTTLIEB, *who plays the part of a bartender for this scene.*)

LONGSHOREMAN   (*Setting the scene for the* ATTENDANT.)

A longshoreman's bar in Astoria, Queens.

(ATTENDANT *gestures for him to proceed.*)

We ought to take our six toughest guys—and the Russians—they take their six toughest guys. Send 'em into a forest—they can have it over there if they want. And the guys that walk out of that forest—that's it.

GOTTLIEB   (*Tending bar.*)

Those Commies would have to shut up.

LONGSHOREMAN   Oh the Russians are All right. If you ask me, they can build a machine as good as America. But fortunately for us, they lack the human people to operate that machine.

GOTTLIEB   You better believe it.

(*A couple enters the bar* WHEELCHAIRED MAN *and* GIRL DANCER. *The* GIRL *puts a quarter in the jukebox — some rock music begins. The* GIRL *starts to dance — in the modern style — quite seductively, in front of* WHEELCHAIRED MAN. HE *snaps his fingers and responds to the music to the best of his abilities.*)

GOTTLIEB   (*Referring to couple.*)

Hey...

LONGSHOREMAN   Yeah...

GOTTLIEB   Ever seen anything like that?

LONGSHOREMAN   No, I never have.

(THEY *watch the couple awhile.*)

LONGSHOREMAN   Watch this.

(*He approaches* COUPLE, *speaks to* GIRL.)

Say, miss...

GIRL DANCER   Yes...

LONGSHOREMAN   (*Referring to fellow in chair.*)

All systems are not go...

GIRL DANCER   (*Still dancing.*)

I don't fellow you…

LONGSHOREMAN   You know…the astronauts…all systems are not go. Wouldn't you rather move around with a guy whose systems are all à go-go?

WHEELCHAIRED
MAN   (*Talking through a throat box, as though the victim of a tracheotomy.*)

Why are you harassing us? We were behaving peaceably.

LONGSHOREMAN   I hadn't noticed.

(HE *grabs* GIRL.)

C'mon, baby, let's move around a little…

(GIRL *moves half-heartedly.*)

WHEELCHAIRED
MAN   You've just made a serious mistake, fella.

LONGSHOREMAN   That right?

WHEELCHAIRED
MAN   That's right. First of all…

(HE *switches off throat box and speaks in a normal tone.*)

I don't really speak that way.

(*Twirls off whiplash collar.*)

Second of all, I don't wear this… Third of all…

(*Getting to his feet and kicking off braces.*)

I don't need these. Last but not least…

(*Whipping off his shirt to show a well-muscled frame and huge championship belt.*)

…silver-belt karate, the highest karate level of all…

(*With three quick moves,* HE *wipes out* LONGSHOREMAN, *who falls to the floor. At a certain point in the* WHEELCHAIRED MAN'S *metamorphosis, it has become apparent that* HE *is* BIEBERMAN.)

ATTENDANT

(*Delighted at the discovery.*)

Hey! Bieberman! … You wipe him out and then you and the chick leave…

BIEBERMAN

That's right.

ATTENDANT

How many times you get away with that stunt?

BIEBERMAN

Twenty-five times. Sarah and I started to do it every Friday night, as a form of social involvement, a means of smoking out society's predators…

ATTENDANT

But you kept getting away with it. I forget, what are you doing here?

BIEBERMAN

An Arab at the 92nd Street YMHA dropped a 200-pound barbell on my neck.

ATTENDANT

That's right. And don't you forget it…. All right, everybody, that does it… You told some pretty good stuff, but we got to make room for the next crowd.

(*Gesturing toward second door.*)

… Everybody in there… We enjoyed having you, sincerely.

BROKER

All the exercise – the steam – what good did it do?

ATTENDANT

What are you complaining about – you're in the best shape of your life…

BROKER	That's true. Well, I'll go first. I been finished for a long time.
	(*Hesitates.*)
	Years ago, when you wound up your steambath, there'd be a man outside selling pumpernickel and pickled fish…
ATTENDANT	I'll send some in…don't worry… Now let's go…chop-chop…
	(**BROKER** *goes through the door.*)
1ST YOUNG MAN	Do I look all right?
2ND YOUNG MAN	You look great. It'll be a relief to get out of all that steam.
1ST YOUNG MAN	It's destroyed your hair. Maybe Ralph will be in there.
2ND YOUNG MAN	Ralph? From Amagansett?
1ST YOUNG MAN	He was tacky.
	(**THEY** *go through the door.*)
BIEBERMAN	(*To* MEREDITH.)
	Goodbye. My generation's out of style – I know that – but you'll never know the thrill of having belonged to it.
	(*Starting through grated door.*)
	John Hodiak – hold on, I'll be right with you…
	(**HE** *goes through.*)
ATTENDANT	(*Hollering after departed group.*)
	And if I find any candy wrappers I'll send Gottlieb in there to kick your ass.

(*Only* TANDY *and* MEREDITH *remain.*)

TANDY
Kick your ass, kick your ass… I'm supposed to respect that? … Where's the grandeur? …the majesty…?

ATTENDANT
I'm saving that for the next group that's coming in. I hear they got some terrific broads. They're single. Bunch of nurses. They fell from a cable car… I'm going to hit them with all this grandeur and majesty…

(*Goes over to console, which appears in the mist.*)

Start a new rock and roll group called Grandeur and Majesty…

(*Console blips back its response. To* MEREDITH.)

You goin', lady?

MEREDITH
(*Hesitating.*)

Well, as I was telling Mr. Tandy, I've only recently had my first orgasm…and I haven't paid my Bloomingdale's bill. I've never been to Nassau in the Bahamas…

ATTENDANT
First orgasm…good-looking girl like you… Must have been a slip-up. Maybe you been having them all along and didn't realize it… All right, let's go, you two… I got a lot of cleaning up to do…

TANDY
I told you I'm not accepting this.

ATTENDANT
You want me to get rough?

TANDY
How would you like it if you were in the middle of a great Chinese restaurant…you've had your spareribs, a little soup – you're working up a terrific appetite and bam! You're thrown out of the restaurant. You never get to enjoy the Won Shih pancakes.

ATTENDANT   I can get any kind of food I want up here...except lox. The lox is lousy, pre-sliced...the kind you get in those German delicatessens... I can't get any fresh lox... I don't know why that is...

TANDY   It's like a guy about to have some terrific operation. The odds against him surviving are ridiculous, Newton High School against the Kansas City Chiefs. They're working on his eyes, ears, nose, throat, and brains. A whole squadron of doctors is flown in from the Caucasus where they have all these new Caucasus techniques. He's hanging by a hair - and, miracle of miracles, he makes it. Gets back on his feet, says goodbye to the doctors, goes home, and gets killed by a junkie outside of Toots Shor's... That's the kind of thing you want me to accept.

ATTENDANT   That's a pretty good one.

(*Takes a note on it.*)

I'm gonna use that... Yes, come to think of it, that is the kind of thing I want you to accept.

TANDY   Well, I can't. I worked too hard to get where I am... You know about Wendy Tandy, my ex-wife...

ATTENDANT   Good-looking broad, I know about her...

TANDY   That stunt she pulled?

ATTENDANT   That was a good one... Gottlieb, you got to hear this...

(GOTTLIEB *comes over.*)

TANDY   (*More to* MEREDITH *than anyone.*)

She's an unfaithful wife. Fine. You put up with it, you don't. I did. Fair and square. So then we meet a retired hairdresser who has become an underground film-maker. He shoots his film through those filters of teased hair...it's a new technique. This is the guy Wendy falls madly in love with. And she moves out – to live with him. Fair and square. She prefers him, she's got him. Swingin'. I'm getting along fine – got a few deals of my own cooking – and all of a sudden I get an invitation to go see a film that this hairdresser has put Wendy in – down on Charles Street. And I find out – in one of the Village papers – that what he's done is make a huge blow-up in one of the scenes – I don't know how to say this – of her private parts. It's very artistic, don't get me wrong... The audience thinks it's a Soviet train station...

MEREDITH   God, I'd never do that. How did he get her to do that? She must have really loved him.

ATTENDANT   Hey, Gottlieb, what did I tell you?

(GOTTLIEB *hangs his head.* HE'S *shy.*)

TANDY   Well that makes me the supreme schmuck, cuckold, whatever you want to call it – everybody agreed? Half the city sitting in a theatre, looking at my wife's box – sitting inside it, for Christ's sakes...

MEREDITH   For heaven's sake, what did you do?

TANDY   That's what I'm getting at. The old me would have come in with guns. I'm a very good shot – at under seven feet. There's a technique I learned over at the Academy. You run into a little room after this cornered guy and as you shoot you're supposed to start screaming

(*Demonstrates.*)

YI, YI, YI, YI, YI, YI. That's in case you miss, you scare the shit out of him. But I finally figured, what the hell, it's nothing to do with me. She's that kind of a girl. I knock off this guy, the next one'll be Xeroxing her pussy all over Times Square. So I said the hell with it and I went to the movie.

MEREDITH   How was it?

TANDY   Not bad. As a director, the guy had some pretty good moves. It fell apart in the middle, but it was worth seeing. I sat in the balcony... But you see, I got past all that baloney. Out in the clear, after ten years... and I started getting straight in other areas, too. I got a wonderful, calm girlfriend... We could be sitting at McGinnis' restaurant and Fidel Castro could walk in. She'd stay calm, low, even, maybe give him a little smile. I love that. I never had it... And then I forgave my mother...

MEREDITH   For what?

TANDY   I never liked the work she was doing. She ran a chain of dancing schools in Appalachia. She'd talk these starving families into taking mambo lessons...very bitter woman. Anyway, I took her out of Appalachia, got her an apartment in White Plains, and I like her now. She's seventy, and all that iron has dropped out of her.

GOTTLIEB   (*To* ATTENDANT.)

Any more sexy parts?

ATTENDANT   Shut up, Gottlieb. I think that's wonderful the boy's nice to his mother. I didn't know that...

(*To* TANDY.)

What else you got…?

TANDY	I just kept ironing out all the wrinkles in my life. The toughest thing, believe it or not, was leaving my art-appreciation job over at the Police Academy. I really thought the dicks would kill me if I left. They didn't. They gave me a wonderful send-off party. They hired a little combo – four convicted forgers – and they ran some Danish art films they'd confiscated at a Bar Mitzvah in Great Neck. And then at the end my art students gave me a replica of Michelangelo's David – seventy-five bucks over at Brentano's… Only one fellow gave me any trouble, detective named Flanders, said if I left he'd trail me all over the world, any place I tried to hide – and hunt me down like a dog.

(DETECTIVE FLANDERS *appears, gun in hand.*)

FLANDERS	Tandy…
TANDY	(*Running.*)

Jesus…

ATTENDANT	You kidding? Don't worry about this guy.

(*Gestures and* FLANDERS' *gun turns to a milkshake.*)

All right now, get in there.

(FLANDERS *goes through the door.*)

TANDY	That was close.
MEREDITH	I'm glad he's on our side.
ATTENDANT	You see, I told you. And you said nasty things about me. You called me a bad guy…

TANDY	Anyway, you get the idea. I've gotten my whole life on the right track for the first time. I don't hate Wendy. I'm doing this wonderful work for brain-damaged welders. You ask the welders what they think of me. And I've got a marvellous new girl who's got this surprising body. You look at her face you just don't expect all that voluptuousness. You say to yourself, she's a little girl, a quiet little girl, comes from a nice family, where did these tits come from…?
ATTENDANT	Hey, hey, there's a lady…
MEREDITH	Oh, that's all right. I don't mind tits. Knockers is the one I don't care for.
TANDY	All right, excuse me, but do you get the idea? I got everything bad swept out of the room. I'm closer than ever to my daughter. That trip to Vegas really brought us together. I'm doing work that I love. Warner Brothers saw the first hundred pages of my Charlemagne book and I understood they like it for Steve McQueen…
ATTENDANT	Twentieth is going to buy it…for Charlton Heston…
TANDY	Then you admit…you admit I'm getting out of here.
ATTENDANT	They're going to buy it from your estate…
TANDY	Look, I'm all clean and straight and honest. I got rid of all the garbage. Any crooked lines, I erased them and drew them straight… I don't hate anybody. I love a lot of people. I'm at the goddamned starting line. I'm ready to breathe clean air. I tore myself inside out to get to where I am – and I'm not taking up anybody's space. I'm ready to cook a little. Swing. What kind of fellow is that to snuff out?
ATTENDANT	A good fellow. But I'm snuffing him out anyway.

TANDY   Where's your compassion?

ATTENDANT   I do plenty of good things. Half the things I do are good, maybe even a little more. That's right, maybe even a little more. Nobody notices them. I never get any credit, but I do plenty of good things. I make trees, forests, soccer fields. I let hernias get better...

TANDY   But you'll wipe out a guy like me...and a lovely blonde girl like that...

MEREDITH   Oh, listen, the blonde part shouldn't enter into it, I can see that.

ATTENDANT   I let you go, I got to let the next guy go. Pretty soon nobody's dead. You'd have people coming out of your ears. Have you seen Istanbul lately? Downtown Istanbul? Los Angeles?

MEREDITH   I'd never live in L.A. I don't think there's one sincere person in the whole city.

ATTENDANT   Let me ask you something. While you were doing all those things, unloading your old lady, you know, straightening out your head, how did you feel?

TANDY   Good. Excited...it was like being in a whirlpool bath. An emotional whirlpool bath. It even made my body feel good; it got springy and toughened up...

ATTENDANT   There y'are. You felt good, you had a whirlpool bath...a springy body... Need I say more?

TANDY   You don't understand something. I probably never made it clear. This is very important to me. We're talking about my life. I'm not asking you for seats to a hockey game.

ATTENDANT   (*Mocking.*)

	It's very important to him. Nobody else is alive.
TANDY	Is there anything I can do for you?
ATTENDANT	You got to be kidding. You do something for me? What in the world would God want?
TANDY	A sacrifice? …burnt offering…?
ATTENDANT	(*As though* HE *is finished with* TANDY.)
	I got no time to fool around. I got a whole new crowd coming in.
TANDY	That's it? You're going through with this? Well, I'll tell you right now, if you're capable of wiping out a once-confused fellow who's now a completely straight and sweet guy, then I got no choice but to call you a prick.
	(*To* MEREDITH.)
	I'm sorry.
MEREDITH	Oh, that's all right. You can say prick. Pecker is the one I don't care for.
ATTENDANT	(*Astonished.*)
	God? … Did I hear you correctly? … Can I believe my ears? … Blasphemy…?
TANDY	That's right. If you're capable of doing something like that. Taking a fellow to the very threshold of marvellous things, teasing him along and then ace-ing him out just when he's ready to scoop up one lousy drop of gravy – that is bad news, I'm sorry…
ATTENDANT	I'll tell you right now nobody ever called me that. That's bad, boy, that is low. Wowee… That's what I call sinning, baby. You're in real trouble now. You have put

your foot in it this time, fella... You going to stick to what you called me? ...that dirty name? ...talking that way to God?

TANDY   Yeah, I'm going to stick to it...and you know why... because when I was in that Chinese restaurant...and I lost my breath, and I had no feelings, and I was numb and white, as white as a piece of typing paper, and I said over and over and over I don't want to die, I don't to want to die, I don't want to die...and told you, in my way, how much I treasured every drop of life – you weren't impressed, you didn't hear a whisper of it...

ATTENDANT   That right, Gottlieb? Did he do that?

               (GOTTLIEB *nods*.)

TANDY   I thought you knew everything.

ATTENDANT   Almost everything. Once in a while there's an administrative error. Anyway, I did hear you. You came over a little weak, a little static thrown in there, but I hear you. That's why you're here. Otherwise... (*Pointing to grated door*.)

               ...you'd have gone straight in there...

TANDY   Then not everybody comes here...?

ATTENDANT   Neurotics, freaks...

               (*Contemptuously*.)

               ...those with stories to tell.

TANDY   How was mine?

ATTENDANT   Not bad. I heard worse.

TANDY   You were touched... You just won't admit it.

(HE *advances, threateningly.*)

Now let me out of here.

ATTENDANT   You come near me, I'll send you back with cancer, then you'll know real trouble.

(TANDY *grabs* GOTTLIEB, *wrestles him to the floor, holding him around the neck, threatening him with his other hand.*)

TANDY   All right, talk, and be quick about it. Otherwise, you get these carpet tacks right in your face. How do we get out of here?

ATTENDANT   You talk, Gottlieb, and I'll see to it that you never work again. What can he do with a lousy bunch of carpet tacks?

GOTTLIEB   I don't know. But I'm not taking any chances... Get a mirror.

MEREDITH   (*Reaching into a purse.*)

I've got one here.

GOTTLIEB   Shine it in his face. He can't stand that.

(SHE *hesitates, then does.*)

ATTENDANT   (*Cringing, trying to hide.*)

Take that away. I don't want to see myself – a homely guy with pockmarks.

TANDY   (*Releasing* GOTTLIEB, *deflecting* MEREDITH'S *mirror.*)

All right, wait a minute, I can't go through with this... Leave him alone...

ATTENDANT   (*Gets himself together – then, as though feelings are really hurt.*)

Et tu, Gottlieb…

(*Makes a move to* MEREDITH, *indicating it is her turn.*)

MEREDITH   Au revoir, Mr. Tandy. Did I do All right with the mirror?

TANDY   You did fine, kid.

(MEREDITH *goes through the door.*)

ATTENDANT   (*To* TANDY.)

You couldn't stand that, right, to see God get wiped out… It gave you a funny feeling.

TANDY   I don't like to see anybody get wiped out… I'm notorious for breaking up fights… I once threw a guy through the window of a furniture store because somebody was picking on him and I didn't want him to get hurt.

ATTENDANT   You got a lot of nice qualities… Too bad I'm filled up. I'd let you work around here for a while… Listen, what are you giving yourself such a hard time for…? Suppose, for a second, I let you out of here… What would you do…?

TANDY   What would I do? … Are you kidding? … What is this, a put-on? … You didn't hear me go on about my new life? The exciting world that's out there waiting for me? … This terrific new quiet girlfriend who practically brings me the newspaper in her teeth, who watches me like a hawk for the slightest sign of sexual tension, and then whop – she's in there like a shot to drain it off and make me feel comfortable again… And if I feel like going out at four in the morning to get some eggs – she's right there at my side – because she comes from a tradition where the man is like a gypsy king and the woman is someone who drags mutton to him on her back, all the way up a hill. And all she ever hopes for is that he'll throw her a lousy mutton bone while she's sleeping in the dirt at his feet... And this is an intelligent girl, too...a Bryn Mawr girl... When I'm alone with her...

ATTENDANT

You like this girl...?

TANDY

Like her? ... Oh, I see what you mean... Yeah...if I'm so crazy about her, how come I'm constantly chasing chicks all over the place? ... All right, I'll admit to you that she's a little on the quiet side – that sometimes all that quiet drives me nuts... All right, let's face it, she's basically a dull girl. Terrific kid, loyal, faithful, brings you mutton, but the sparks don't fly... And it did cross my mind that maybe I'll find another girl who's got a little more pizzazz... I'll give you that...

ATTENDANT

Another girl...

TANDY

Yeah. Another girl. Oh, I got ya', I got ya' – a new one isn't going to be the answer either... As delicious as she looks now, in two months I'm a little restless again... And that's the way it's got to be if I live to be a hundred...

(*Trails off.*)

Look, I got to travel... I got to move around. And I'm all set to get rolling. There was a woman who used to take care of me when I was little and she was born in Mukden, during the...Chinese war... Very interesting woman, had a lot to do with my future development. Well she used to describe a beautiful church to me where she went to school, right in the middle of Mukden. I always promised myself I'd get over there and see that church, maybe carve my initials in one of the pews... And that somehow that would round off the corners on Mrs. Grainger's life... She's got a spinal condition... I still write to her. Well, I can do that now. I can go right over to Mukden and stand in the middle of that church...

ATTENDANT   She wants you to go to Mukden...

TANDY   ...Oh, I see what you're driving at – I don't have to go to Mukden. I don't have to go 26,000 miles and break my balls to show her I love her. I can stay right here and carry out some of the proverbs she taught me and it's just as good... You got a point there... All right, forget Mukden... No more Mukden... I got friends, terrific friends. We hang around this bar called The Quonset Hut, run by a dyke, a rich retired dyke. We hang around there, sometimes till five in the morning, talking about Milton and the Brontë sisters. These friends of mine are terrific people – they're a little screwed up in their personal lives – most of them have been divorced three or four times – but very often those are the best people, the ones who get divorced over and over... Anyway, I want to do a lot more of that – hanging around this dyke bar till five in the morning with my divorced friends, talking about Milton and the Brontë sisters... And I have to get back to my book. Now I know what you're going to say and I'm way ahead of you – that I have no real visceral interest in Charlemagne – that I just picked that subject because it has a prestige sound to it. Well, you're wrong. To me it's just a loosening-up process, a way of warming up the writing muscles so I can be ready for the real book I want to write on – Vasco da Gama and the Straits of Magellan.

(*Weak little laugh as though aware* HE'S *told a joke. No response from* ATTENDANT.)

No, seriously...you have to get the muscles limber... What you're saying is if I really wanted to write I'd stop crapping around with Charlemagne... I see what you mean... You get more prestige from a truly observed book about...cheeseburgers than you can from a schlock Charlemagne book... Boy, you really nailed that one down... I'll tell you what, let me smoke a cigar, All right?

(*Takes one out.* ATTENDANT *has sat down and begun to arrange the cards for a game of solitaire.*)

I get these from Switzerland from a guy who brings them in from Cuba. It costs a little extra, but it's really worth it. They say you're supposed to stop smoking these when you get about half way down, but I don't know. Sometimes I think the last half of the cigar is the best part. I can tell a Havana cigar in one puff. It's not the tobacco so much as the rolling process they use. They have a secret rolling process that nobody's ever been able to pry away from the Cubans... If it kills me I got to get back and have some more weekends with my daughter. Those weekends are the most beautiful part of my life now. I mean there's no more hassle...no more crazy marriage in the background... It all gets telescoped down to just me and her, hanging around together.

(*Looks at* ATTENDANT *for response, doesn't get one.*)

...So you're asking me how come I'm always going crazy thinking up places to take her... How come I'm always dragging her to puppet shows...? Well, all I can say is that it's the city's fault... Where the hell are you supposed to take a kid in the city...? If we were out on a farm, it'd be a different story... But I do see what you mean – Jesus, you really know how to zing it in there...what you're driving at is that I have to keep taking her places because I actually have nothing to say to her... Maybe I don't even like kids... She'd be better off staying home and hanging around with a pack of little girls...

(*Handling cigar.*)

A guy once told me the reason for the special flavour of these Havana cigars is that the tobacco is supposed to be rolled on the thighs of Cuban women... Jesus, wouldn't that be something...?

I got to get out of here... I got to get out of here... I got things to do...

(ATTENDANT *continues his game of solitaire – the last sound heard is the flicking of the cards....*)

CURTAIN

SARDINES

A LOVE STORY ABOARD
THE SPANISH ARMADA

CHARACTER LIST

ANNOUNCER	The narrator of the play, using an authoritative voice (BBC-style).
PHILLIP II	King of Spain.
DON PEDRO FERRARA	A young emissary who comes from a long line of naval heroes.
THE DUKE OF MEDINA SEDONIA	A 38-48 years old man whose hair is turning white. He is married to Dona Maria. He reluctantly takes over as Commander of the Most Fortunate Fleet after Santa Cruz suffers a heart attack.
DONA MARIA MENDOZA	A 10 years old girl, wife of the Duke of Medina Sedonia. She has a remarkable aptitude for finance and takes care of the Duke's financial affairs. This role is best played by a gawky adult.
QUEEN ELIZABETH I	Queen of England.
SIR FRANCIS WALSINGHAM	Queen Elizabeth's chief advisor.
SIR FRANCIS DRAKE	Commander of the British Fleet, thought of as one of the greatest navigators the world has ever known and has never lost a battle. He is in love with Antonia.
DIEGO	Sir Francis Drake's black manservant.
DONA ANTONIA NAVARRE	A chronicler that documents the Duke's deeds on his voyage. She had a relationship with Francis Drake, and accompanied him on his celebrated around-the-world voyage. She has magnificent burnished hair, and her philosophy is "what goes unrecorded never occurred."
FRANCESCA	Dona Maria's child friend.
PARMA	A man with a long white beard and a mad look in his eyes. He gives up helping the Spanish in

the Armada to focus on the riddle of the Dutch inland irrigation canals.

DWARF A savage-like man played by the tallest member in the company.

SIGNOR GIAMBELLI A dapper little man who has an odour of garlic. He is a genius who is relocated to England to build hell-ships.

MCLAGHLIN
MCCABB "Thane of the Savage Mountain." A burly, savage-looking individual.

OLD MAN A savage-like man wearing a stovepipe hat and a green coat.

ADDITIONAL CAST German Woman, Seamen, Clansmen, Aide, Servant, First Seaman, Second Seaman, First Nobleman, Second Nobleman, Victualler.

ANNOUNCER (*Off Stage*)

> In the late Sixteenth Century, Spain held sway over a mighty Empire – and why should it not have? Its influence ranged from Portugal to the Netherlands to Peru, to the West Indies, Lithuania, and other ungodly corridors of the globe. Flushed with triumph, PHILLIP II set out to build the greatest naval armada the world had ever known. This is the story of the Spanish armada, the man who led it, the strange circumstance under which he was chosen to command, and his adventures, both romantic and otherwise, as they might have happened. It has been suggested that the fate of the Armada holds a lesson for us in our own troubled times. The author doubts this, but is willing to be convinced.

ACT ONE

ANNOUNCER (O.S.)   1588…The Escorial…Palace of the Spanish King

(*A dark corner of the Throne Room.* PHILLIP II, *on his knees, is working on state papers, scribbling in the margins of some, affixing the royal seal to others.*)

(HE *becomes aware of* DON PEDRO FERRARA.)

PHILLIP   You may approach the throne, Don Pedro.

DON PEDRO   Thank you, your Grace. I have good news. The Armada is completed.

PHILLIP   Splendid. How many ships does it include?

DON PEDRO   One hundred and fifty, your Grace. The greatest naval force ever assembled in history.

PHILLIP   I could not be more delighted. Now refresh my memory. What exactly did we plan to do with it?

DON PEDRO   Your Grace thought we might sail it through the Channel and bring England to its knees.

PHILLIP   Of course. How foolish of me to have forgotten. Tell Santa Cruz we move at once against our enemy.

DON PEDRO   I'm afraid that's impossible. The hero of Lepanto is dead.

PHILLIP   But that's absurd. I saw him only a fortnight ago, and he had colour in his cheeks.

DON PEDRO   A bit too much, it would appear. When the Armada was in formation, and the last urca had taken up its position, the poor man clutched at his chest and pitched forward into Lisbon Harbour.

PHILLIP   What a pity! How he loved that Armada.

DON PEDRO   Adored it.

PHILLIP   Spent seven years of his life, tossing it together.

DON PEDRO   Unfortunately, he'll never get to enjoy it.

PHILLIP   Not where he is now.

                        (*Beat.*)

                        Send his widow a little something.

DON PEDRO   I'll attend to that.

PHILLIP   Not too extravagant.

DON PEDRO   Of course not.

PHILLIP   Well…we can't just have an Armada, bobbing about in
                        the harbour – depleting our poor treasury. Who else do
                        we have to command?

DON PEDRO   Your Grace might want to consider THE DUKE of
                        Medina Sedonia. Quite well respected and comes from
                        a long line of heroic figures.

PHILLIP   Yes, but has THE DUKE himself ever done anything
                        heroic?

DON PEDRO   When Sir Francis DRAKE attacked our garrison at
                        Cadiz, it was THE DUKE who rode to the rescue.

PHILLIP   Arrived a bit late, as I recall.

DON PEDRO   Yes, but the troops were delighted to see him. And he
                        may have put a hole through DRAKE's galleass.

PHILLIP   (*Perking up.*)

                        Was this verified?

DON PEDRO

The hole was – but some say it was punched through by a disgruntled Walloon.

PHILLIP

(*Knowingly shakes his head.*)

Those Walloons.

(*Recalls.*)

Medina Sedonia. It's coming back now. Marquis of Cazaza in Africa and twelfth Senor of Sanlucar de Barrameda. Grows oranges in Andalusia and married a ten-year-old. He may be just the fellow for us. Was the marriage ever consummated?

DON PEDRO

Apparently not. The bride found him unsophisticated.

PHILLIP

I like the sound of this fellow. I'd always wanted someone a touch less worldly than Santa Cruz. Never could get through to him. Cancel that gift to his widow.

DON PEDRO

Of course.

PHILLIP

And inform Medina that he is now the Commander of the Most Fortunate Fleet. I want him at the mouth of the Tagus in a fortnight.

DON PEDRO

I'll notify him at once. Would your Grace himself care to inspect the Armada?

PHILLIP

(*Waving him off.*)

No, no, I'm sure it's in excellent repair. And I have an Empire to look after. This morning alone I have to eliminate heresy in the Low Countries, bring our sheep back from Portugal and concoct a plan to upset the Germans. Irritating bunch, aren't they?

DON PEDRO

They *are* Germans.

PHILLIP

That would account for it... Now go and see the Duke and let me get on with my kingdom.

(DON PEDRO *bows his way out.* PHILLIP *lifts his seal, looks about for a document, finds it, gives it a little stamp, hits his own hand.*)

(DON PEDRO *walks across stage and finds* THE DUKE OF MEDINA SEDONIA *clipping away at an orange bush, outside his villa.*)

THE DUKE

But I don't *want* to lead an Armada. I know very little about them and wouldn't have the faintest idea of what to do with one. Tell his Majesty I'm terribly flattered – I kiss his hands, I kiss his feet – but I don't particularly *like* Armadas.

DON PEDRO

I'm afraid Phillip has made up his mind.

THE DUKE

Explain to him that I'm past my prime. I'm anywhere from thirty-eight to forty-eight, depending upon which account you find trustworthy. I'm weak in the knees. Just a few days ago, I had my first dizzy spell and fell forward into one of these bushes. Fortunately, I was discovered by a passing hidalgo who took me by the shoulders and said "You're all right, do you hear. There's absolutely *nothing* wrong with you." But I don't know that hidalgo. He's a strange hidalgo. How do I know I can trust him? Look at my hair. It's turning white, and I can't decide whether to touch it up or not. What do you think?

DON PEDRO

Seems fine.

THE DUKE

Thank you. I can't possibly leave now. I have a ten-year-old wife. You know what they're like at that age. Changing every second. Need constant attention...

There are taxes to be collected... And the Fig Festival is just around the corner. So is the Date Festival, come to think of it. Can't afford to miss that... And I've never been to sea. The very mention of water makes me ill. I have to eat sardines blindfolded. I'll make a fool of myself. So be a good fellow and find someone else. Try the Mayor of Castile. Excellent chap and I understand he loves armadas.

(*Looking O.S.*)

Who's that grim-looking fellow you've brought along?

DON PEDRO   The military solicitor.

THE DUKE   (*Dismissively.*)

I'm certainly not going to *sign* anything.

DON PEDRO   He's also the executioner.

THE DUKE   I see.

(*Puts his arm around* DON PEDRO.)

Suppose I drop around and have a look at this armada of yours. Tell me about the compensation.

DON PEDRO   The King was hoping you would contribute a million maravedis.

THE DUKE   But that's virtually my entire fortune.

DON PEDRO   There's a strong chance the Pope will reimburse you when you set foot in England.

THE DUKE   Will he send an advance?

DON PEDRO   No, no, we tried that. Couldn't budge him.

(*Hands* DUKE *a thick document.*)

Here's a folio that will tell you all you need to know about leading an armada...

THE DUKE   (*Takes it.*)

Must weigh a ton... Is it any good?

DON PEDRO   It picks up after a few hundred pages...

THE DUKE   I may have to skip around...

(DON PEDRO *exits.*)

(THE DUKE *pages through the folio, reading faster and faster, then flings it aside, and stands before a glass, fluffing up his beard, getting into a greatcoat.*)

(DONA MARIA *enters, stands beside him in her nightgown, sleeping cap.*)

DONA MARIA   Why can't I go along?

THE DUKE   Because you're ten years old. Ten-year-olds don't belong on an armada. They belong at home where they're nice and safe. Besides, I only said I'd have a *look* at the armada.

DONA MARIA   Yes, but I know you. You'll like it and I'll be left behind.

(*Thinks.*)

If you accept the commission it will be *your* armada, won't it? And you'll be able to take along anyone you like.

THE DUKE   That's not quite true. The King specifically said: No wenching.

DONA MARIA	Wenching? What's this got to do with wenching? We don't wench here. Why would we wench on the armada?
THE DUKE	Strange things happen on the high seas. Now, off you go to bed. You can hop up on my shoulders and play horsey.
DONA MARIA	(*Spiteful.*)
	Don't be absurd!
THE DUKE	But you love horsey.
DONA MARIA	That's not true. I *never* loved horsey. I pretended to love horsey because it meant so much to you. Horsey was your world. I *hated* horsey.
THE DUKE	(*Head in his hands.*)
	If only I'd known…
DONA MARIA	And there's a German girl who'll be aboard the armada. She's already set up house on a Flemish hulk.
THE DUKE	That's impossible. I'm sure there's an explanation.
DONA MARIA	She's having an affair with a Latvian bilge skimmer.
THE DUKE	(*Grimace.*)
	…Charming… I'll look into that as soon as I get to Lisbon.
DONA MARIA	What will I do when you're gone?
THE DUKE	Lots of things. You can collect taxes. You've always enjoyed that… You can clean up your room.
DONA MARIA	Don't be absurd.

(*Beat.*)

I'll have an affair. You'll see. There are lots of people who like me – ones you don't know about.

THE DUKE   (*Wearily.*)

Dona Maria Mendoza, will you *please* act your age. As a loyal subject of the King, I'm merely going to inspect a few ships. Even if I *were* to lead the armada, it wouldn't take forever. All I'd have to do is bring England to its knees, and I'd return immediately.

(*Sighs.*)

Why I ever got involved with a ten-year-old is beyond me.

DONA MARIA   You didn't talk that way when we were courting.

THE DUKE   You were an entirely different person when you were four.

(DON PEDRO *appears, nods to* DONA MARIA *and then half carries, half drags the protesting* DUKE *to the edge of the Harbour.*)

DONA MARIA   (*Holds on to his leg, wailing, cursing in Spanish.*)

Let him go... Asillipollao... Abadesa... Aquebado

(*When she can no longer hold on, cries out.*)

ASQUEROSO.

THE DUKE   (*Looking back.*)

I should never have married that child. What got into me...?

DON PEDRO   She has some charm.

THE DUKE	Not when you live with her... But look here, I've only said I'd pop round and have a look at the Armada. My colleagues tell me it's in wretched condition.
DON PEDRO	The King will have your ships keened and tallowed, add on several Portuguese carracks and replenish your stores. But the men are getting restless.
THE DUKE	But I'm not at all ready for this. If I could take a small boat out to the pond...get accustomed to the water... proceed in stages...
DON PEDRO	There isn't time for that.

(THE DUKE *looks out, hears voices of a throng of a seamen, awaiting him.*)

THE DUKE	Oh my God, there are thousands of them out there. What on earth will I say to them?
DON PEDRO	It's not terribly important. They just want to have a look at you. But do try to be inspiring.
THE DUKE	(*Sneezing.*)

I've caught a chill, too. I knew that would happen.

(HE *pulls himself together, clears his throat, starts vamping, making up his address as he goes along.*)

Men of the Armada, it's good of you to come. Many of you have signed on for this great enterprise, not quite knowing its function. Let me enlighten you. Our purpose is to sail against England and, once there, to free oppressed Catholics.

FIRST NOBLEMAN	Forgive me, your Grace, but my information has it that the Catholics are quite happy.

SECOND NOBLEMAN	Nonsense. I have a cousin in Marylebone who's miserable.
FIRST NOBLEMAN	I'm familiar with that cousin of yours. He's *always* been miserable…
SECOND NOBLEMAN	Mind your tongue or prepare for a good thrashing…
FIRST NOBLEMAN	You bloody popinjay…

(*As* THE DUKE *tries to calm them, a whole cacophony of voices is heard – much like a wild press conference, questions overlapping.*)

"Does Phillip intend to assume the English throne?" "Will the Portuguese stand by us?" "They never have before… Why should they now?" "What about my wool?" "You and your bloody wool…" "I haven't heard a word about taffeta. Will taffeta be taxed?" "Who'll keep an eye on the Germans?"

THE DUKE   (*Trying to restore calm.*)

Now, now, gentlemen, I'm sure all of your conflicts will be resolved once we're out on the high seas. If I may, a word about the Armada itself… Each of you has his own little function and you are not to be faulted for failing to grasp the full scope of this affair. It's quite a large armada, some one hundred fifty ships in all, give or take a pinnace or two. We have culverins, semi-culverins, all sorts of culverins, which I'm told will be useful. Among us are Biscayans, Andalusians, Castilians and a sprinkling of Italians…all flung together in what we trust will be one big happy fighting force. Also along are our galley slaves whose function will be to push forward five times, pull back six.

(*Demonstrating.*)

Forward five, back six. Do try to remember that. Among the many falsehoods spread by Elizabeth is that we'll be taking along 3,000 wet nurses to care for the babies of slaughtered Englishmen. This, of course, has no basis in fact. We have our friars who can perform that function. We're not going to be an overly strict armada, but we're not going to be a casual armada either. There are certain rules to be adhered to. No wenching, of course. All women are to leave immediately or face being tossed unceremoniously into the sea once we set sail. I refer particularly to a certain German woman.

(*Looks out.*)

You know who you are.

VOICE (*SHOUTS O.S.*)   Nein! Nein!

THE DUKE   Just run along.

(*Continues, gathering confidence.*)

No personal daggers and no continuation of feuds. If you've despised one of your shipmates for years, you're to stop doing so immediately. You can, of course, resume detesting this individual once we're back in Lisbon... Contrary to rumor, we *are* going to be paid, not as much as some of us would like, but a tidy little something... The King assures me that God is on our side and finds the English distasteful... One last item: Before his untimely death, the late Santa Cruz allotted three sardines a day per man. I've raised that to six...

	(*Folds some notes.*)
	(*A great "HURRAH" from the crowd.*)
SEAMAN	(*Lone dissenter.*)
	Six? Only six? How's a man to sustain himself on a bloody six sardines?
THE DUKE	They're quite large. Some of them run at least a foot long. I'm sure you'll be pleased... Now I believe that covers it.
	(*Suddenly thrusts out a fist and shouts.*)
	FOR GOD AND COUNTRY!
	(*Great roar of approval from the assemblage; the stage fills with brilliantly coloured flags, pennants and banners of the Armada...castles of Castile, dragons and shields of Portugal, cross and foxes of Biscay...* THE DUKE*'s own Banner – a red St. Andrews cross on a snow-white field... Appropriate music.*)
THE DUKE	(*U.S. through the pandemonium.*)
	How did I do?
DON PEDRO	Quite nicely. The raised fist was particularly inventive.
THE DUKE	I just tossed that in. And what did you think of our family crest?
DON PEDRO	Which one was that, your Grace?
THE DUKE	(*In disbelief, slightly offended.*)
	The red St. Andrews cross...on a snow white field...
DON PEDRO	Oh yes, of course, your Grace. It stood out prominently.

THE DUKE	I should hope so. I paid a fortune for it…
DON PEDRO	It was well worth every peso…
DUKE	(*Pacified.*)
	Now look here, you're not going to abandon me, are you? I need a capable seaman.
DON PEDRO	Actually, I've never been to sea either.
THE DUKE	Oh… But shouldn't I have *someone* along who's had a bit of experience?
DON PEDRO	There's no question it would be useful. I do come from a long line of naval heroes. And I *have* been boning up.
THE DUKE	(*Perks up.*)
	Then you'll join me?
DON PEDRO	Wouldn't dream of missing it.
THE DUKE	Splendid.
	(*They embrace. Then* THE DUKE *looks out.*)
THE DUKE	(*Turning colour.*)
	Oh my God, the water.
	(HE *faints.*)

ANNOUNCER (O.S.)   England. Elizabeth the Queen, and her chief adviser,
                   Sir Francis Walsingham.

ELIZABETH   So they're coming, are they?

WALSINGHAM   I'm afraid so, your Majesty. They've made little progress
                   thus far, but they give every indication of being on their
                   way.

ELIZABETH   It's Mary Stuart and that awful head of hers that did it.
                   I knew we shouldn't have put that woman to death. We
                   could have kept her locked up for decades…and now
                   they're coming…with their garlic and their hulks and
                   their wet-nurses…all because of that head… You're
                   sure you've disposed of it?

WALSINGHAM   Quite sure, your Majesty.

ELIZABETH   Then why do I see it each night, rolling toward me
                   across the tiles at Fotheringay…

                   (*Imitates head, rolling.*)

WALSINGHAM   A Spanish trick perhaps.

ELIZABETH   I *told* you not to put her on the block.

WALSINGHAM   You asked only to be spared the details. It was the same
                   with the Irish spies at Smerwick. We strangled them
                   one by one and kept it from you.

ELIZABETH   But you're telling me now.

WALSINGHAM   Yes, I suppose I am.

ELIZABETH   No matter. Where will they land?

WALSINGHAM   The Margate people think Margate, the Poole people
                   Poole, and in Ness, they feel it's Ness for sure.

ELIZABETH	Ness? Why Ness?
WALSINGHAM	Why not Ness?
ELIZABETH	I suppose you're right. But they *are* coming.
WALSINGHAM	They give every indication of doing so.
ELIZABETH	(*Intoning.*)
	Well, let them come. I may appear before you as an old woman, a specter of my former self, the thinnest suggestion of an individual, a wisp of a thing...
	(*Carried away.*)
	a shell...a husk...
WALSINGHAM	(*Impatient.*)
	Now, now, you're no husk...
ELIZABETH	Thank you...
	(*Rises.*)
	And let them not be misguided... I have the heart and soul of a lion...let them come...
WALSINGHAM	I believe they're coming whether we permit them to come or not.
ELIZABETH	(*Not hearing this.*)
	...and fear not, England. I shall be your sword and musket, I shall be your powder and pike. There on the beaches, I shall greet them, there shall I slay the first garlic-eater who dares to tread upon your hallowed soil. I shall defend you to the last...for you are England... and I am...

(*After some thought.*)

I am England, too.

(*Lets this sink in, then takes* WALSINGHAM'S *arm and becomes chatty.*)

Now you're *sure* they're coming...

WALSINGHAM   (*Exasperated as* HE *leads her off.*)

Yes! They should be here any day now.

ELIZABETH   Not necessarily. They might call it off. One never knows... But you've disposed of that head?

WALSINGHAM   Absolutely.

ELIZABETH   There'd be hell to pay if anyone found it.

(*Imitates severed head.*)

ANNOUNCER (O.S.)   On Deck… The Duke's flagship…San Martin.

(THE DUKE *is peering through a spyglass, strains forward as if* HE *sees something, leans a bit further, then abandons the effort.*)

THE DUKE   (*Flinging spyglass over his shoulder.*)

Can't see a bloody thing.

(*A loose cannon comes rolling toward him across the deck and pins him against the railing.*)

(DON PEDRO *comes to his assistance and the two struggle to push it away.*)

THE DUKE   (*Struggling.*)

Shouldn't this be latched to something?

DON PEDRO   (*Straining.*)

The men haven't quite mastered the technique…they're working on it…

THE DUKE   Ask them if they'd mind doubling their efforts…as a special favour to the Commander.

(THE TWO MEN *send the cannon rolling off in another direction.*)

THE DUKE   (*As he recovers.*)

I should have paid attention to the signs. They were all wrong for this voyage. The week we left, it rained blood in Norway. I don't place much stock in such reports, even if it were a few drops.

(*A pair of seamen appear, carrying long pole-like weapons on their shoulders.*)

FIRST SEAMAN	What do you want done with these pikes, your Grace? They're beautifully crafted, but our men are too short and squat to hurl them at the English.
THE DUKE	Can't they be broken in two?
FIRST SEAMAN	I don't believe so, your Grace.
THE DUKE	Then just slide them under something for the time being. I'm sure we'll find some use for them.
FIRST SEAMAN	As you wish, sir.
	(SEAMEN *go off.*)
THE DUKE	(*Frustrated.*)
	If it isn't one thing. …The odds on the Paris Bourse are seven to one we'll never see Cornwall…we've been sailing our hearts out for a month and we haven't even moved in the right direction. What would his Majesty say if we just chucked it…?
DON PEDRO	The command would be turned over to Don Oquendo, a great favourite of the King.
THE DUKE	(*Encouraged.*)
	And I'd be sent home.
	(*Reads* DON PEDRO'S *expression.*)
	I *wouldn't* be sent home.
	(*Reads it some more.*)
	He'd have my head…
DON PEDRO	I'm afraid so, your Grace.
THE DUKE	Why does he always have to have someone's head?

DON PEDRO	It's his nature. He can't help himself. Except for that one flaw, he's been an excellent king.
THE DUKE	It's quite a flaw.
	(*Takes a deep breath, brightens.*)
	The sea air *is* invigorating… And I suppose there's nothing wrong that a favourable wind won't cure. We can put in at Corunna, revitalize and be off to face Sir Francis Drake. What do you know of him?
DON PEDRO	It's been said that he's bold, fearless, bloodthirsty, has never lost a battle and is probably the greatest navigator the world has ever known.
THE DUKE	Apart from that…
DON PEDRO	That's pretty much it.
	(*Thinks.*)
	I suppose he does have one weak spot.
THE DUKE	Oh, good. Tell me quickly.
DON PEDRO	He's a bit self-conscious about his humble origins. As a boy, he had to hang his laundry out on the bowsprit of a beached frigate.
THE DUKE	Did it dry?
DON PEDRO	Not entirely.
THE DUKE	How awful. And I have just the plan. We'll circle his flagship and remind him of his childhood laundry.
DON PEDRO	That should bring him to his knees.
THE DUKE	(*Hands him a spyglass.*)

Why don't you take the watch. I'm not quite sure I know what I'm watching for anyway.

(THE DUKE *starts below, trips over an emaciated seaman who has crawled out on deck.*)

THE DUKE   Forgive me, you poor man. I didn't see you. Take my cloak. You're shivering.

(*Removes his cloak.*)

SEAMAN   I don't need your cloak. What good would that do? And what happened to the sardines you promised us?

THE DUKE   I didn't like the looks of them. The eyes were cloudy. I've called for a fresh shipment. They should arrive in a month or so.

SEAMAN   And what do we do in the meanwhile?

THE DUKE   I'll speak to the cook... I'm sure he'll be able to whip up a little something. I saw some old biscuits lying around in the galley.

SEAMAN   I never should have signed on for this voyage. My wife warned me against it.

GERMAN WOMAN   (O.S.)

Ja ja...

THE DUKE   (*Aloud, to himself.*)

I thought we got rid of her...

(*To seaman.*)

And if *that's* your attitude...

(HE *snatches back cloak, goes below.*)

ANNOUNCER (O.S.)   On deck, the St. Bonaventure, flagship of SIR FRANCIS DRAKE.

(DRAKE *is dining alone.* DIEGO, *a Cimmarone, attends to him and scans the horizon.*)

DRAKE   My compliments, Diego. You've set an excellent table.

DIEGO   Thank you, Sir Francis. Is the hen to your liking?

DRAKE   The hen is fine, but it's the table I find satisfying.

(*Lifts a goblet.*)

The Royal seal...the ivory crest...

(*Reflects.*)

You know, I wasn't born to luxury. As a youth, I had to hang my laundry on the bowsprit of a beached frigate.

DIEGO   So you've indicated, Sir Francis.

DRAKE   It never really dried, either.

DIEGO   I hadn't realized that.

DRAKE   You have no idea what it's like to walk about in damp gaiters...

DIEGO   Must have been dreadful.

DRAKE   But of course you never faced that problem in the Bastimentos...

DIEGO   No, we didn't, sire.

DRAKE   Wore no gaiters at all, most likely.

DIEGO   None at all, sire.

DRAKE	You're lucky. But that's all history. Has the Armada been sighted?
DIEGO	Our scouts report they're floundering off the coast of Corunna, and they seem a bit heavy in the water.
DRAKE	That's good. It's a sign they're carrying gold.
DIEGO	More likely taffeta.
DRAKE	I'm not interested in taffeta.
DIEGO	Nonetheless, they might be carrying it.
DRAKE	They'd better not be. If they're carrying taffeta, I'm calling off the whole enterprise.
DIEGO	I understand, sire.
DRAKE	Don't mention taffeta again.
DIEGO	Of course, your Grace. Although I do feel obligated to point out that the fabric is mentioned in young Will Shakespeare's new play.

(*Recites.*)

"A fair hot wench in flame-coloured taffeta..." Part One, Henry IV.

DRAKE	I didn't realize that. But I don't want to hear any more about it.
DIEGO	Of course, your Grace...
DRAKE	(*Can't quite let go.*)

Lady Drake wore taffeta for her bridal gown. It was coarse to the touch.

| DIEGO | I believe your Grace said the same of Lady Drake. |

DRAKE   (*Snaps.*)

              Never mind.

              (*Calms himself.*)

              Are we upwind?

DIEGO   Yes, sire.

DRAKE   Make sure we stay that way.

DIEGO   Indeed, sire.

DRAKE   It's impossible to lose a battle if you're upwind.

DIEGO   I'm aware of that, sire.

DRAKE   That's why I like to remain that way.

DIEGO   Of course.

DRAKE   You may have an hour of leisure.

DIEGO   Thank you, Sir Francis.

DRAKE   Ever wonder why I'm so racially tolerant?

DIEGO   It did cross my mind, sire. Might it be that I've been
              loyal, faithful, led you to every significant treasure on
              the Spanish Main, done all of the circumnavigation on
              your trip around the globe and seen to it that you got
              full credit for your exploits and I received none?

DRAKE   That has nothing to do with it.

DIEGO   Of course, your Grace.

              (*Begins clearing table.*)

              Forgive me, Sir Francis. May I ask a personal question?

DRAKE   All right.

DIEGO   Here we are on what promises to be your greatest
                 triumph. Shouldn't you be filled with bluster and good
                 cheer?

DRAKE   I'm never filled with bluster and good cheer.

                 (*Thinks.*)

                 Bluster occasionally. Good cheer never. Surely you
                 know that.

DIEGO   (*Cautiously.*)

                 You're not, perchance, upset about the woman?

DRAKE   Antonia Navarre? I do think of her now and then...
                 How can she possibly ignore me?

                 (*Lists triumphs.*)

                 I've been knighted by the Queen, there's a 25,000 ducat
                 bounty on my head... I'm considered a *God* in the
                 Moluccas.

DIEGO   (*Tinge of scorn.*)

                 The Moluccas. You know what we say about the
                 Moluccas in the Bastimentos?

DRAKE   (*Snaps.*)

                 No, and I don't care. Be off with you...

                 (DIEGO *bows, leaves.*)

DRAKE   (*Calls after him.*)

                 And remember to stay upwind. I refuse to fight anyone
                 unless I'm upwind.

(*Aloud, but to himself.*)

And I don't understand that woman.

(*We see him, in a dream-like sequence, begin to dance a tango with the beautiful Antonia Navarre... After a few turns, she hesitates, seems doubtful, runs offstage.*)

DRAKE   She turned her *back* on me? What was she thinking?

ANNOUNCER (O.S.)   The cabin of the Duke…

(HE *sits, unsteadily, at a wooden table.*)

VICTUALLER   (*Entering with a tray.*)

Some fortifying broth, your Grace.

THE DUKE   Thank you. And do try to hold it steady. It makes me
ill – when it pullulates.

VICTUALLER   Forgive me, your Grace, but don't you mean 'undulates'?

THE DUKE   Either one. And what's the bloody difference? There's
no need to be grammatically precise when I'm out here
on the high seas.

VICTUALLER   I think there is.

THE DUKE   You're a victualler. Stick to what you know. And
incidentally, isn't there another term for your
occupation.

(*Pronounces it.*)

Victualler. It hardly comes trippingly off the tongue.

VICTUALLER   (*Tries one.*)

Poop-deck assistant?

THE DUKE   (*Considers.*)

We'll stay with the other.

(THE VICTUALLER *trips, spills broth on* THE
DUKE'S *lap.*)

THE DUKE   Oh, for God's sakes.

(HE *leaps up.*)

VICTUALLER	(*Attempts to dab at him.*)
	I'm terribly sorry, your Grace. Let me get you another.
	(VICTUALLER *opens cabin door. Cannon rolls in.* THE DUKE *braces himself.* VICTUALLER *steps between him and the cannon, stops forward motion.*)
	(*With great effort,* VICTUALLER *reverses its direction, sends it rolling back out the door, slams door shut and stands there, breathing heavily.*)
VICTUALLER	That should be the last of it.
THE DUKE	(*Still dabbing at wet uniform.*)
	I wouldn't be too sure.
VICTUALLER	Let me help you.
	(VICTUALLER *reaches for a cannon cloth overhead. It falls on the Duke's head, envelopes him – like a tent.*)
THE DUKE	(*Struggling to get free.*)
	This isn't going to work out. Don't you have an assistant, someone who isn't quite so fidgety?
VICTUALLER	I've been trying so hard to please.
THE DUKE	That may be the problem. All that effort…
	(*A little suspicious.*)
	How long have you been victualling?
VICTUALLER	As far back as I can remember. I come from a long line of victuallers. My father actually died victualling.
THE DUKE	I'm sorry to hear that. He probably didn't care for the work.

(*Comes closer.*)

What *is* it about you? You're not like the usual Armada crowd.

(*Circles round, suddenly reaches forward and tears off* VICTUALLER'S *blouse. More than obvious it's a woman.*)

I knew it. And what a nice set of juicy *grande buca chichigonzagas.*

VICTUALLER   (*Trying to cover up.*)

What a perfectly dreadful expression.

THE DUKE   It's common naval usage. Been around for centuries. I'm personally opposed to it, but as Commander, it's essential that I blend in and demonstrate that I'm an Armada type.

(HE *removes* VICTUALLER'S *headpiece.*)

THE DUKE   (*Wondrous.*)

And hair too.

(*Suddenly smitten.*)

Magnificent burnished hair...such as I've never before touched...as fragrant and intoxicating as my beloved groves at Andalusia...

(*Stiffens.*)

No matter. I'm forced to have you put ashore on a cockeboat.

VICTUALLER
(ANTONIA.)   Surely there's another name for it.

THE DUKE   I'm afraid I have no time to muck about with linguistics.

ANTONIA   (*Defiant.*)

                    Then go ahead – put me ashore in a

                    (*Wincing.*)

                    cockeboat.

THE DUKE   You're right. It does have a jarring sound to it. Why do
                    you look so familiar?

ANTONIA   (*Introduces herself, shakes out her hair fully.*)

                    Dona Antonia Navarre.

THE DUKE   That's not helpful.

                    (*Recalls.*)

                    I remember. You were at Cadiz, the day I arrived a bit
                    on the late side. You're a chronicler, aren't you?

ANTONIA   A novice – although Lope de Vega did say I had
                    promise, if only I were to find a worthy subject and sink
                    my teeth into him…

                    (*Corrects herself.*)

                    …it.

THE DUKE   I enjoyed what you wrote about me.

                    (*Recalls.*)

                    "The Duke arrived late to battle, was totally ineffectual,
                    but behaved throughout with dignity."

ANTONIA   Actually, de Vega helped me with that section. But you
                    are a hero of mine and I'd like to chronicle your deeds

on this voyage. After all, if they go unrecorded, it's as if they never occurred. New Philosophy.

THE DUKE   Old rubbish. And why the disguise? Why didn't you introduce yourself properly?

ANTONIA   I thought you might have put me ashore in one of your

(*Winces.*)

cockeboats… And besides, I like disguises.

THE DUKE   You're very strange. And I'm afraid there aren't going to be any great deeds. All I want to do is avoid disgrace. You can't be a hero at my age.

ANTONIA   That's nonsense. What about the current Doge of Venice? Ninety years of age and blind. Yet as we speak, he's off sacking Constantinople.

THE DUKE   I know about the Doge. He has some vision in his right eye. His story *is* inspiring, but I'm afraid you'll have to look elsewhere. I'll probably arrive late anyway.

ANTONIA   I like that in you. My last lover was a Biscayan. Kept arriving early.

THE DUKE   It's been a year since we almost met. But I never stopped thinking about you.

ANTONIA   I had no way of knowing. You made no effort to find me.

THE DUKE   I was shy.

ANTONIA   That's not your reputation.

THE DUKE   It's inflated.

ANTONIA	The other chronicles warned me about you. "Stay away from him," they said. "He's a spoiler."
THE DUKE	Where did they get that idea?
ANTONIA	Henriette de Guise? … Henriette St. Cloud? … Henriette Touraine?
THE DUKE	Brief, trivial encounters…
ANTONIA	All of them your lovers…all of them ruined for other men.
THE DUKE	That's highly doubtful.
ANTONIA	They say you have a young wife.
THE DUKE	Yes, I suppose you could describe her that way.
	(*Dismissive.*)
	It was one of those arranged things.
ANTONIA	Who arranged it?
THE DUKE	Actually, she did. She arranges everything. It's one of the nice features of this Armada. A little peace and quiet.
ANTONIA	What prompted you to take up with her?
THE DUKE	I wish I knew. We met at the Pistachio Bazaar in Seville.
ANTONIA	How *is* that? I've always wondered.
THE DUKE	…if you like pistachios… She came toddling out of the crowd and there was something about her carriage that made her seem wise beyond her years. I bought her a licorice stick…and before I knew it, we were exchanging marriage vows…

ANTONIA   Surely her parents objected.

THE DUKE   On the contrary, they were delighted to get rid of her.

ANTONIA   Yet you've remained together.

THE DUKE   She showed a remarkable aptitude for finance. My affairs were a mess. She had them straightened out in no time.

ANTONIA   Why not leave the child and retain her as your accountant?

THE DUKE   I may have to... But there was more...

               (*Remembers fondly.*)

               She spoke the language of another generation...

ANTONIA   Of four-year-olds?

THE DUKE   That's just it. I soon saw that she had nothing to teach me. Whenever she spoke, I heard my own words coming back at me.

ANTONIA   Still, that's quite an achievement for a toddler.

THE DUKE   Perhaps. But now that I've met you I can see the enormous advantage of being with a grown woman.

ANTONIA   I'm not sure I can survive all of this flattery...

               (*Beat.*)

               Why didn't you pursue me? The truth now.

THE DUKE   It's a bit delicate.

ANTONIA   I insist on knowing.

THE DUKE   (*Proceeding cautiously.*)

When I saw you at Cadiz, you were wearing embroidered gaiters...

ANTONIA   (*Explaining.*)

It was the day of the Wine Festival.

THE DUKE   ...the sun hit you at a narrowing angle...and I thought you might be a bit insubstantial in the...stern...

ANTONIA   (*Reaching for her bottom.*)

Oh...

THE DUKE   (*Reassuring.*)

But now that I've seen you again, I realize I *couldn't* have been more wrong...

ANTONIA   What?

THE DUKE   It's boorish of me, but it *was* an issue and I'm delighted it's been settled in a favourable manner.

ANTONIA   So am I, I can assure you.

THE DUKE   (*Disposing of the subject.*)

Now...What did you do after Cadiz?

ANTONIA   Roamed the Continent...

(*Looks around at her bottom.*)

You're sure you're satisfied?

THE DUKE   Quite. Go on.

ANTONIA   I can always jump overboard.

THE DUKE   No, no, it's fine.

ANTONIA	I wrote some alehouse jingles at Cologne. One of them correctly prophesied the Plague.
THE DUKE	I missed that one.
ANTONIA	It was very well received. I worked for a mercury dealer for a period – and then I accompanied Sir Francis Drake on his celebrated round-the-world voyage.
THE DUKE	(*Impressed.*) You chronicled Drake?
ANTONIA	That was my intention. But I grew disenchanted with him at Tierra del Fuego. He falsified the number of days it took him to cross the Straits of Magellan.
THE DUKE	It was announced as fourteen.
ANTONIA	It was actually forty. But all that mattered to him was that he beat Cavendish.
THE DUKE	Forty isn't bad.
ANTONIA	I agree. But there were other matters. His alleged hatred of Phillip when all he cared about was Spanish gold. When he locked Reverend Doughty in a Slaughter Box and tied him to the mainmast, I decided he wasn't a fitting subject for me. I commandeered a bark at Valparaiso and made my way back to Lisbon.
THE DUKE	…missing a chance to chronicle the greatest sailor of our age.
ANTONIA	Nonsense. He has a manServant named Diego who does all of his circumnavigation and he's never even given him so much as a co-credit.
THE DUKE	The swine.

ANTONIA

He was only interested in me for my money.

THE DUKE

That's doubtful…and I didn't realize that chroniclers were wealthy.

ANTONIA

We're not *poor*. Besides, I'd never stopped thinking about you, either. When I heard you'd been chosen to lead the Armada, I decided to steal aboard and tell *your* story.

THE DUKE

A celebration of failure.

ANTONIA

I see no evidence of that. But if you persist in presenting yourself that way, others will happily agree.

THE DUKE

I'll try to reign myself in. And let's not lose each other again.

ANTONIA

Never.

(THEY *seem to embrace –* SHE *draws back, unfurls a long, long sheet of parchment, whips out a quill pen and sits back, poised.*)

ANTONIA

Shall we begin? What is your plan when you finally face the mighty fleet of Sir Francis Drake?

THE DUKE

It's a bit fuzzy. My instructions are to avoid Drake if possible and rendezvous with the Duke of Parma. He has 30,000 troops at his disposal. Somehow we're to ferry them across to England, and we're all to invade the British Isles together.

ANTONIA

Where will this rendezvous take place?

THE DUKE

Who knows? Flanders. Calais. After all

(*Romantically.*)

it *is* a rendezvous.

(*With that,* HE *grabs parchment, furls it back, takes pen out of her hand and throws it overboard.*)

ANTONIA   (*Distressed.*)

That was my favorite pen…

THE DUKE   (*On fire.*)

I'll get you another…

ANTONIA   (*Still upset.*)

It was taken from a dying swan and immersed in hot ashes to give it flexibility. It was the third quill……
They tried to give me the first, but I insisted on the third…

THE DUKE   I told you I'd replace it…

ANTONIA   Where are you going to find a dying swan?

THE DUKE   I'm sure there are plenty around… And this isn't about quills and swans…

(*Passionately.*)

We've lost an entire year. If I hadn't been chosen to lead the Armada… If you'd been stopped at the harbour… If the wind hadn't forced us to revitalize at Corunna… If the king…

ANTONIA   (*Impatient.*)

Yes, yes, I quite get your point… And I so miss having my pen…

THE DUKE   (*Snaps momentarily.*)

Will you stop going on about that pen…

(*Softens.*)

I want to show you my house in Montenegro, where the olive trees, impossibly, come bursting out of the concrete.

(*Beat.*)

Actually, it's in litigation…

(*Loses himself.*)

Costly business. Although it's my solicitor's feeling that there may be a possibility of a settlement…

ANTONIA   (*Tapping him on the shoulder.*)

Your Grace…

THE DUKE   Oh, yes…

(*Passionate again.*)

Who knows what lies ahead in the Channel. We may never have this chance again. And it isn't as if we've just met. This is a *second* encounter. I've got to have you.

ANTONIA   (*Panicked.*)

NO!

THE DUKE   Oh.

ANTONIA   It isn't that I don't want to. I've thought of little else since the day I first saw you at Cadiz – wide-eyed, befuddled.

THE DUKE   Late, too. Let's not forget that. Just *once* I arrived twenty minutes late and I've never heard the end of it.

ANTONIA   I don't care about that. It could have been an hour and I would have loved you all the more. But I'm a serious chronicler. I don't want to write doomsday forecasts all my life. To be sure, it's financially rewarding, but I want more. To get it, I'll have to look at you with cold eyes…

THE DUKE   You don't have cold eyes…

ANTONIA   Then I'll *get* them. Don't you see — if we made love, it would *be* there in the work, bursting out of every quatrain.

THE DUKE   You honestly feel it would have that much impact?

ANTONIA   Every bit…

THE DUKE   Then perhaps we *should* reconsider…

ANTONIA   Here's my proposal… Why don't I start? I'm never really comfortable until I plunge in…

(*Significantly.*)

And then the moment we spot England.

THE DUKE   (*Perks up.*)

Now *there's* a suggestion.

(SHE *picks up tablet, realizes she doesn't have her pen.*)

THE DUKE   (*Offering her another.*)

Try this. It's from a goose.

ANTONIA   Dying?

THE DUKE   Enfeebled…

ANTONIA   Third quill?

THE DUKE   (*Reluctantly.*)

Second…

ANTONIA	(*Dismissive.*)
	Oh, well…
THE DUKE	Will you at least try it?
ANTONIA	(*After giving pen a doubtful look.*)
	You're quite sure Parma is coming…
THE DUKE	It will be most embarrassing if he doesn't.
DON PEDRO	(*Looking in.*)
	Forgive me, your Grace.
	(*Sees* ANTONIA.)
	Signora…the lookout reports a bonfire off starboard. He's fairly convinced it's the coast of Cornwall…
ANTONIA	(*As if amused.*)
	Cornwall…Fancy that…
THE DUKE	Keep an eye out for Drake. I'll be along shortly.
ANTONIA	(*As* DON PEDRO *exits.*)
	Must be lovely this time of year…
	(THE DUKE *advances.*)
	…the lilac…
	(HE *continues.*)
	…the hydrangeas…
	(*As* HE *removes his tunic.*)
	…I didn't.

THE DUKE	You did.
ANTONIA	You wouldn't.
THE DUKE	Wouldn't I?
ANTONIA	What about the Armada?
THE DUKE	What about it?
ANTONIA	Shouldn't it be looked after? It can't very well fend for itself.
THE DUKE	I'm sure it will do very nicely.
ANTONIA	But what if it just flounders?
THE DUKE	What do you think it's been doing all this time?
ANTONIA	But this is different. You've made some headway. It's purposeful floundering.
THE DUKE	I suppose you're right. This Armada has been a nuisance since the day I took it over. Now look what's happened.
ANTONIA	It's only temporary. We've just started up the Channel. Let me do my introduction and I'll join you on deck.
THE DUKE	You promise not to disappear again.
ANTONIA	I promise.

(HE *turns to go.*)

ANTONIA	(*Calls out.*)
	Alonso.
THE DUKE	(*Stops.*)

How did you know that name? It's one of my least publicized names.

ANTONIA   Research.

                   (SHE *runs into his arms.* HE *falls awkwardly, holds his*
                   back, in obvious pain.)

ANTONIA   You poor dear. Are you all right?

THE DUKE   (*Grimaces.*)

                   I'll be fine...

                   (*Reaches for her, stops.*)

                   Are you sure you're not working for the English?

                   (SHE *pulls him to her.*)

ANNOUNCER (O.S.)   On deck…St. Bonaventure…

(DRAKE *and* DIEGO, *scans horizon, using a cross staff and an astrolabe.*)

DRAKE   How many are there?

DIEGO   (*Scans horizon.*)

I've lost count. It's as if the entire city of Madrid were converging on us, bulging with Spaniards.

DRAKE   How appalling.

DIEGO   Good thing we're upwind.

DRAKE   I've always been upwind. I thought you knew that.

DIEGO   Of course, sir.

DRAKE   How do they display themselves?

DIEGO   They're in something of a crescent formation. I've never seen anything quite like it. Thick in the centre and formidable at the ends.

DRAKE   Sounds like Lady Drake.

DIEGO   Sir?

DRAKE   Never mind. Any word from our spies?

DIEGO   Yes, but it's not very encouraging.

DRAKE   Don't tell me. They're carrying taffeta.

DIEGO   It's worse than that.

DRAKE   *Worse* than carrying taffeta?

DIEGO   Dona Antonia Navarre is aboard the San Martin.

DRAKE	As a prisoner?
DIEGO	No. As a chronicler…
DRAKE	She's chronicling the Duke? There's nothing to chronicle. He's failed at every undertaking.
DIEGO	Perhaps that is what attracts her. We have women like that in the Bastimentos. Failure-fouqueres.
DRAKE	(*Doesn't hear this.*)
	It doesn't make sense. I *like* that woman.
DIEGO	Shall we close and grapple with them?
DRAKE	Of course not. You know I don't grapple.
DIEGO	You grappled at San Juan de Ulua.
DRAKE	That was different. I was younger, and we were attacking a defenseless hulk. The Spanish are wonderful grapplers. It's the single thing they do well.
DIEGO	They dance a fine *glosada*.
DRAKE	They *seem* to, but it's all show. Trust me. Technically, they're not very sound. Let me show you their version.
	(*Makes some clumsy moves.*)
	Observe the classic style.
	(*Demonstrates again, perfect.*)
DIEGO	I *knew* there was something wrong with their execution…
	(*Beat.*)
	How shall we proceed?

DRAKE   Stay out of range, pepper them with shots and send out
                      a challenge.

DIEGO   Then you *do* plan to attack.

DRAKE   Not really, but send it out anyway. It can't do any harm.
                      And make surethe Duke receives it personally. You
                      know he once put a hole in my galleass.

DIEGO   I thought it was a Walloon.

DRAKE   That was another hole. It was the Duke's hole that upset
                      me. It was right over my bed. Lady Drake's been rigid
                      ever since. Has the Queen replenished our powder?

DIEGO   No, but she did send an ounce of cologne…as a good
                      luck token.

                      (*Offers his neck for a sniff.*)

DRAKE   (*Sniffs it.*)

                      I'll try some later.

                      (DIEGO *exits.*)

DRAKE   (*To himself, as* HE *holds rail, looks out over water.*)

                      Antonia, Antonia. What can you possibly *see* in that
                      man. Have you tried his oranges? Those horrible pits.

ANNOUNCER (O.S.)   On deck…THE DUKE'S Flagship…San Martin

(DON PEDRO *is at the railing, peering through spyglass.*
THE DUKE *and* ANTONIA *join him.*)

THE DUKE   How do they look to you?

DON PEDRO   Sleek and tight, almost flirtatious in their movements.

THE DUKE   Are you implying that we're fat and dumpy…that no one will ask us to dance?

DON PEDRO   Not at all, your Grace. I just hadn't expected them to be so trim. They're upwind, too.

ANTONIA   Can't we be upwind, too?

DON PEDRO   I'm afraid not. We can't both be upwind. And they were upwind first.

(*Wondrous.*)

But you should have seen our infantrymen this morning, your Grace. All lined up vertically at the mast in their corslets, breastplates, gold-embroidered doublets. Fully armed with their muskets and grappling hooks.

THE DUKE   It must have been quite a sight. And I notice we're in our fabled crescent formation.

ANTONIA   I wondered about that…

THE DUKE   It's essentially a defensive alignment. We can't hurt them…and the best they can do is

(*As it sinks in.*)

pick us off, one by one. We *are* good at it though.

ANTONIA	Best to do something you're good at. And how do you know so much about armadas. It *is* your first one.
THE DUKE	I've been boning up in the wee hours.
	(*An explosive report is heard.*)
ANTONIA	What's that?
DON PEDRO	Drake has flung out another challenge with his usual disdain.
THE DUKE	Why didn't we respond to the first one?
DON PEDRO	I thought it was too disdainful. I just ignored it.
THE DUKE	(*Drawing his sword.*)
	We'll settle *his* cajones.
	(*When* ANTONIA *recoils.*)
	Look, this is an Armada. I can't edit my every epithet.
	(*There is a low rumbling cannonade.*)
DON PEDRO	Drake is signaling some bad news, your Grace...I'm afraid it's of a personal nature. Your wife has left you for a Huguenot.
ANTONIA	(*Going to him.*)
	I'm sorry.
THE DUKE	(*Philosophical.*)
	Oh, well, I suppose it's to be expected. All these months I've spent at sea.
DON PEDRO	Actually, she began the affair the day you left.
THE DUKE	(*Stung.*)

Oh…

(*Musing.*)

A Huguenot. I wonder if I know the fellow.

(*Angrily.*)

How did Drake find out about this?

ANTONIA	He's always been a great one for gossip.
THE DUKE	(*Gestures with sword.*)

Let him draw near. I'll give him something to gossip about.

(*To* ANTONIA.)

We've never lost a pitched battle.

ANTONIA	(*Reminds him.*)

Rio de la Hacha?

THE DUKE	Wasn't pitched.
DON PEDRO	I'm afraid our skill in combat isn't going to count for much. Drake apparently plans to stand out of range and fire his guns, which are superior to ours and obviously don't slide around as much.
THE DUKE	Then how can we grapple with him? We've brought all these grappling hooks from Lisbon.
DON PEDRO	It *is* a bit of a problem. Even worse, we've lost two of our ships. The *Rosario* split its foremast and the *San Salvador* simply blew up.
THE DUKE	Without being hit?

DON PEDRO	A gunner went berserk and threw a flaming faggot into the magazine.
ANTONIA	Oh, dear.
DON PEDRO	They're blaming it all on a dispute over some German woman.
THE DUKE	I knew she'd be trouble. Once and for all, let's get rid of her...
ANTONIA	That's heartless.
THE DUKE	(*Backs down.*)
	At least keep an eye on her.
	(*Reflects.*)
	All these losses and we've barely fired a shot.
	(*To familiar-looking seaman.*)
	Weren't you down with scurvy?
SEAMAN	A slice of lime at Corunna revived me.
THE DUKE	Don't exert yourself. And move. You're in my spot.
SEAMAN	(*Complies, grumbling.*)
	My one chance for glory.
THE DUKE	(*Taking his place.*)
	There'll be plenty of others.
	(*Breathes deeply.*)
	All that spring in my legs. Amazing.
ANTONIA	A whiff of sea air is all you needed.

THE DUKE	(*Getting green.*)
	Don't say that. I'm still pretending we're in the mountains.
ANTONIA	All this harping about infirmity. You're still a young man. With proper care, there's no reason why you shouldn't live another ten good years.
THE DUKE	If only I could believe that.
ANTONIA	I guarantee it.
THE DUKE	(*Suddenly bold.*)
	All right then, El Draque. Let's see if you've still got your crumpets.
	(*Realizes he may have offended her.*)
	Forgive me…
ANTONIA	(*Reassuring.*)
	No, no, it's all right. I rather like that one.
DON PEDRO	(*Excited.*)
	Your Grace, a ship has drawn near. It's only a pike's length away…
THE DUKE	The moment I've been waiting for. I can feel my blood racing.
	(*Appears ready to make a heroic leap, then reconsiders.*)
	That's a fairly big jump. Perhaps we ought to wait until he comes a little closer. Or we could just talk. He probably has some legitimate grievances. I know *I've* got a few.

(ANTONIA *takes* DON PEDRO'S *sword, jabs* THE
DUKE *in the ass with it.*)

THE DUKE   (*Responding.*)

Over the side, amigos, for God and country.

(HE *charges off stage.*)

(*We hear trumpets, the roar of savage battle cries as
infantrymen follow* THE DUKE *off stage. There follows
the clang and clatter of battle, joyous, anguished. Light
and smoke and vibration.*)

(ANTONIA *peers out in the distance. Satisfied with what
she sees, she unfurls parchment. After a suspicious look at
replacement quill, she continues with her chronicle. A dark
shape steals on stage. With a sigh, she shoots this individual,
continues writing through the sounds of battle.*)

(*Another man, weary, soaked, approaches. Resignedly, she
picks up sabre, is about to run him through, sees it's* THE
DUKE.)

ANTONIA   What happened?

THE DUKE   (*Starts to storm off.*)

I'd rather not discuss it.

ANTONIA   But that's not fair.

THE DUKE   (*Gestures toward* DON PEDRO *who also appears,
drenched, exhausted.*)

Speak to *him*. I'm washing my hands of this whole
affair.

(HE *exits.*)

ANTONIA   Don Pedro. What on earth is going on?

DON PEDRO   We've captured the *Santa Ana*.

ANTONIA   But that's wonderful news.

DON PEDRO   Not really. It's one of our own ships.

FREEZE

And black.

ACT II

ANNOUNCER (OFF STAGE)	The Duke's cabin.
ANTONIA	It could have happened to anyone.
THE DUKE	But it happened to me. And it isn't just that I've captured my own ship. In a decade or so, I suppose the shame will wear off. It's what's happened since. We've fired off 134,000 rounds of shots and we haven't hit anything. That's discouraging.
ANTONIA	Well, you *will*. If you keep it up you're bound to hit something. And besides, you shook up one of Drake's key admirals.
THE DUKE	Frobisher? Everyone shakes up Frobisher. The man was a nervous wreck before we got here. You think I took an Armada half-way round the world so I could shake up Frobisher?
ANTONIA	You're being much too hard on yourself. Half your ships are falling apart. You've had to creep along at two knots in foreign waters. With virtually no experience, and a motley little group of provincials, you've held off the superior warships of a great nation.
THE DUKE	Motley? I didn't think we were all that motley.

ANTONIA	Not *motley* motley. What's of primary importance is that you're still *here*.
THE DUKE	Wonderful. We can return to Lisbon and tell the King we were here.
ANTONIA	You're in much better condition than you realize. If Parma joins us with his army, you can both invade England and be right on schedule.
THE DUKE	Perhaps. The trick is to find out his intentions.
ANTONIA	Send a courier.
THE DUKE	Who can I send? I'm the only one whose rank he will take seriously.
ANTONIA	Then go. Disguise yourself as a Moor and be off with you.
THE DUKE	I can't very well leave the Armada.
ANTONIA	Nothing is going to happen to it, I assure you. Nothing's happened to it up to now…nothing will ever happen to it. And the change will do you good.
THE DUKE	You may be right. But before I leave, there's something that's been nagging at me.
ANTONIA	Its nature?
THE DUKE	I realize the fate of an empire is at stake, and if we fail, civilization itself might crumble and wither away. Which makes it all the more difficult to ask this question.
ANTONIA	No, please. Go ahead.
THE DUKE	What is it about me that first attracted you? It was my smile, am I correct?

ANTONIA   (*Hesitates.*)

                 Actually…

THE DUKE   (*Stung.*)

                 It *wasn't* my smile? I don't understand. This smile has
                 always been my strength.

ANTONIA   (*Tentatively.*)

                 It's a nice smile…

THE DUKE   A *nice* smile? I'm afraid you don't understand. The
                 Sedonia smile has been handed down for generations…
                 And you call it *nice*?

ANTONIA   It's *quite* nice. And I hadn't realized it was part of your
                 heritage…

THE DUKE   (*Still shaken.*)

                 I had four teeth put in before we sailed. They were carved
                 from the finest sycamore trees in all of Cordoba…

ANTONIA   And they blend in beautifully…

THE DUKE   They *blend* in?

ANTONIA   No one would ever know they were wood…

THE DUKE   I'm happy to hear that. I paid enough for them.

                 (*Checks his teeth, recovers slightly.*)

                 If it wasn't my smile, what was it?

ANTONIA   (*Thinks.*)

                 Your wit…your intelligence…

THE DUKE   But we never spoke…

ANTONIA   I overheard you chatting with a fruit peddler...

THE DUKE   All we did was discuss fig prices.

ANTONIA   It was the *way* you discussed them. And your carriage.
                     The way you're

                     (*Hesitant.*)

                     constructed.

THE DUKE   (*Gets the implication.*)

                     Do women notice such things? Women of good
                     breeding?

ANTONIA   *Especially* women of good breeding. Enough of that.
                     I'm becoming overheated. Off you go.

THE DUKE   I can't leave in daylight.

ANTONIA   Then let's join the Castilians. They've persuaded a
                     dwarf to dance on the top deck.

THE DUKE   I think I'll miss that.

ANTONIA   You could get started on your disguise...

                     (HE *frowns.*)

                     ... We could make love.

THE DUKE   (*Taken aback.*)

                     I'm not sure if I've heard you correctly. Our guns are
                     hot to the point of exploding. There are sick caballeros
                     sprawled out on deck. Drake has five hundred of his
                     best balls in our side. I'm about to embark on a perilous
                     mission...and you want to make love?

ANTONIA	You're right. It was selfish of me. I finished a canto and thought it would be nice to unwind.
THE DUKE	You finished a canto?
ANTONIA	(*Backing off.*)
	It needs polishing.
THE DUKE	(*Taking her in his arms.*)
	Best to let those cantos sit for awhile.
	(HE *lowers her to the bed, kisses her with passion, is about to make love to her, suddenly stops, sits up.*)
THE DUKE	Where did they find the dwarf?
ANTONIA	He was a galley slave, but he couldn't work the oars. Kept tapping his feet, humming. It was clear he was a born entertainer…

ANNOUNCER (O.S.) Andalusia...the Duke's Villa.

> (DONA MARIA MENDOZA *and her friend* FRANCESCA *appear.*)

FRANCESCA Shall we play King and Queen?

DONA MARIA (*Pacing.*)

No.

FRANCESCA You can be King.

DONA MARIA (*Unappreciative.*)

How ever generous of you.

FRANCESCA What about Marionettes?

DONA MARIA I don't want to play Marionettes. I don't want to play *games*. I'm eleven years old now. I want to live.

FRANCESCA What about your Huguenot?

DONA MARIA He's boring...keeps carrying on about my baby teeth.

(*Mimics.*)

"Can I see zem one more time? ...Flash zem for me... In zat flirty, flirty way." Besides, he has a wife and six children.

FRANCESCA Did he keep this from you?

DONA MARIA No, he told me about them at our first rendezvous. That's what I liked about him.

FRANCESCA Any news from the Duke?

DONA MARIA Be serious. Why should he contact me? He has his Armada and he's having all that fun. And I know what he's *doing* out there, too.

FRANCESCA	Not wenching?
DONA MARIA	Of course wenching. Why do you think he left?
FRANCESCA	To wench?
DONA MARIA	What else?
FRANCESCA	He'll be back in a year. You can wench with him.
DONA MARIA	Oh, shut up. I'll be an old woman by then.
FRANCESCA	Just one quick game of Hearts.
DONA MARIA	Out of the question.
FRANCESCA	Let's have a staring contest.
DONA MARIA	You'll cheat.
FRANCESCA	You can't cheat at staring.
DONA MARIA	(*Stares back.*)
	You're cheating now. And besides, I have to finish these stupid taxes.
	(S H E *begins going through ledgers, folios.*)
FRANCESCA	If you've lost interest in your Huguenot, do you mind if I see him?
DONA MARIA	Yes…
	(*After a pause.*)
	If I tell you something, will you promise never to repeat it to anyone?
FRANCESCA	All right.

DONA MARIA	Before the Duke left, I peeked into his chambers one morning, and I saw his staff.
FRANCESCA	The cook? The gardener? You see them every day.
DONA MARIA	No, you ninny. His *staff*. He wakes up with it in the morning, when the blankets become unraveled…
FRANCESCA	(*Sees what she's getting at, reacts with horror.*)
	AAAAGHHH.
	(SHE *goes flying out of her room.*)
DONA MARIA	(*Aloud, to herself.*)
	I'll have to get another friend.

ANNOUNCER (O.S.)   *An irrigation ditch in the Netherlands.*

(*Some marsh-weeds... Hip deep in them is* PARMA, *who consults a chart, looks out in the distance. Beside him is* THE DUKE, *soaked, in a MOOR disguise which he has thrown together, doesn't really work... .*)

PARMA   Tell me again, who are you?

THE DUKE   (*Patient, though frustrated.*)

Medina...Medina Sedonia... I'm here with the Armada. The Spanish Armada? We've come all the way from Lisbon...by sea...

PARMA   (*Scanning horizon, consulting chart.*)

Oh, yes...the Armada... How's that venture coming along?

THE DUKE   We're *here*... After much hardship, we're actually *in* the Channel... Docked outside Calais...Phillip assured us you'd bring your armies out to join us and we'd all invade England together.

PARMA   *Who* said that?

THE DUKE   Phillip... The Second... The King...

PARMA   Oh, yes...how is he?

THE DUKE   Fine.

PARMA   Has quite an Empire, hasn't he?

THE DUKE   Yes...and he'd like to expand it...which is why he sent us all this way...to join you...

PARMA   And *your* name, sir?

THE DUKE   Medina Sedonia...

PARMA	Oh yes, the Armada chap. Well look, the whole idea is absurd. I can't imagine why Phillip sent you on this goose chase. Invade England? An entire country? All those lovely people living there... Must be some mistake...
THE DUKE	I can show you my instructions...
PARMA	Don't bother. Now look here. I've become fascinated by the Dutch inland irrigation system. Whoever is the first to make sense of it has a guaranteed place in the history books. Give up this Armada nonsense and join me in a truly noble venture – trying to puzzle out the riddle of the Dutch inland irrigation canals. What do you say?
THE DUKE	Under normal circumstances...
PARMA	Then you'll do it. Excellent. I knew I could count on you.
	(*Points outward.*)
	Observe the way this sluice appears to be going in one direction when it's actually going in quite another.
THE DUKE	Yes, I see.
PARMA	You see? How can you see? Even the Dutch can't see, you idiot. Who are you, anyway? State your business and be off with you.
	(*Grabs him.*)
	But before you go, answer one question.
THE DUKE	What's that?
PARMA	Any word on the Armada?

ANNOUNCER (O.S.)   Drake's flagship, the St. Bonaventura.

DIEGO   The Duke is in a dreadful condition, Sir Francis. He's made a fruitless trip to Parma and captured his own ship.

DRAKE   And the woman?

DIEGO   Still at his side, scribbling away.

DRAKE   (*With contempt.*)

He's a *garlic*-eater.

DIEGO   They say garlic has certain aphrodisiacal powers.

DRAKE   Nonsense. I tried a clove and it did nothing for me.

DIEGO   (*Dismissive.*)

A clove.

DRAKE   I don't want to discuss garlic. Tell Elizabeth I want a Giambelli hell-ship in the harbour as soon as possible. And make sure it's a Giambelli.

DIEGO   They're a bit expensive.

DRAKE   I know that...and they're worth every peso...

(*To himself.*)

A *garlic*-eater.

(*A sallow light. A dwarf does a sad little sailor's dance... A flute accompanies him. Lights down... Faded cheers are heard.*)

ANNOUNCER (O.S.)   *Above Deck… The San Martin.*

                    (ANTONIA *paces anxiously, looks out to sea.*)

                    (THE DUKE *staggers onstage, soaked, of course. A mess.* SHE *runs to him.*)

ANTONIA   Are you all right? You look awful.

THE DUKE   My feet are a bit damp. Other than that, I'm fine. How was the Dwarf?

ANTONIA   He was wonderful. So sad. But he seemed a bit tall…for a dwarf.

THE DUKE   They're coming in all sizes these days…

ANTONIA   And they're still considered dwarves?

THE DUKE   Oh, yes. Unless you're a dwarf aficionado.

ANTONIA   I'm certainly not that… And I missed you.

THE DUKE   I missed you, too.

ANTONIA   I thought about nothing but our love. You pushed me this way, you arranged me that way… Have you ever done choreography?

THE DUKE   Dabbled a bit.

ANTONIA   I knew it. Will Parma bring his armies out to join us?

THE DUKE   I doubt it. He's insane.

ANTONIA   The poor man. Is there anything we can do for him?

THE DUKE   He's getting along very nicely. *We're* the ones who need help. Any word from the oppressed Catholics on the Mainland?

ANTONIA   Not that I know of.

THE DUKE   Not even a frail wave of approval? We came all this way
                  to liberate them.

ANTONIA   Perhaps they're too oppressed to wave.

THE DUKE   This is quite a fix. No Parma. No Catholics. All these
                  preparations to invade England and we've no one to
                  invade it with.

ANTONIA   What about your sailors?

THE DUKE   We're better off sending the dwarf.

ANTONIA   'We still have the Armada. And we have each other.

THE DUKE   For the moment.

                  (*With dramatic portent – as a heavy chord is heard.*)

                  I haven't told you about Giambelli's hell-ships.

                  (*The announcement startles her.* HE *puts his arm around
                  her.*)

THE DUKE   I'm sorry. I didn't mean to frighten you.

ANTONIA   You certainly acted as if you did. What *is* a Giambelli
                  hell-ship?

THE DUKE   It's a ghostly craft with no men aboard, just powder and
                  a clockwork fuse. All it has to do is brush against us and
                  we're done for – especially if we're flammable.

ANTONIA   Are we?

THE DUKE   I'm afraid so.

ANTONIA   How come the Armada doesn't have its own hell-ship?

THE DUKE   We couldn't afford Giambelli. But don't be alarmed. We
                  do have a defence.

ANTONIA	Yes?
THE DUKE	He might miss us.
ANTONIA	That is encouraging, but even if it doesn't, I'm not really afraid. We'll just resume our love in the afterlife.
THE DUKE	You don't believe that rot, do you?
ANTONIA	With all my heart.
THE DUKE	What form does it take?
ANTONIA	Whoever does first waits for the other. The two then live together – eternally.
THE DUKE	I believe it, too.
	(THEY *cling to each other.*)
THE DUKE	I just hope it's not an *authentic* Giambelli.
ANNOUNCER	(O.S.)
	The throne room of the queen.
	(ELIZABETH *confers with* WALSINGHAM. GIAMBELLI *is off to one side, waiting, as if for a decision.*)
ELIZABETH	How much does he want for them?
WALSINGHAM	Ten thousand pounds.
ELIZABETH	Each? He must be insane. Who does he think I am, the Pope? Tell him I'll give him five and not a penny more.
	(WALSINGHAM *confers in whisper with* GIAMBELLI *who seems displeased, then returns to Elizabeth's side.*)

WALSINGHAM   He feels it's an insulting figure. He'll *do* it, of course, but for him to perform his best work...to get a true Giambelli hell-ship...

ELIZABETH   I'll not be bullied. That's my final offer.

(*Stops WALSINGHAM.*)

On second thought, tell the little greaser to peddle his scallions elsewhere.

WALSINGHAM   (*Diplomatic.*)

May I remind your Majesty that Signor Giambelli is a genius. The Siege of Antwerp would have been a farce without him. And he specifically relocated to England to build hell-ships.

ELIZABETH   He's a garlic-ball. How dare he dictate terms to me.

WALSINGHAM   I thought your Majesty rather enjoyed a touch of garlic now and then.

ELIZABETH   Yes, but these people virtually bathe in it.

(*Leaves, shivering with revulsion.*)

(WALSINGHAM *sighs, goes to confer (*in Italian.*) with* GIAMBELLI.)

GIAMBELLI   (*After listening.*)

I haven't eaten garlic in years...

ANNOUNCER (O.S.)   *On Deck... The San Martin... Furious wind, storm.*

DON PEDRO   We're awfully close to the shoals, your Grace. I suggest we put in at Calais.

THE DUKE   I thought of that. The Mayor said he was happy to have us in the area but preferred that we stay offshore and wave as we go by.

ANTONIA   He did send over a bowl of fruit.

THE DUKE   Have you tasted it? The good fruit went over to Drake.

ANTONIA   The swine. What's your next move?

THE DUKE   It depends on the wind, actually. Drake won't approach us. We can't very well fly across the water and attack him. Small wonder Parma went insane. Maybe I'll go insane, too, and you can take command.

ANTONIA   With pleasure. A mighty Armada that, for all one might criticize it, has never broken formation. I'd be proud of that, even if I were defeated.

THE DUKE   Don't say 'defeated.' Why is everyone in such a rush to be defeated?

(*Sound of popping rockets.*)

DON PEDRO   Hell-ship off starboard, sir.

THE DUKE   Is it a Giambelli?

DON PEDRO   I don't know, sir. It's my first hell-ship.

THE DUKE   This is our darkest moment. Get a pinnace out there and try to steer it away from us...

DON PEDRO   (*Cracks, for the first time.*)

Get a pinnace, get a zebra, do this, do that… I'm only one man.

THE DUKE   Don Pedro…I'm astonished.

DON PEDRO   (*Hangs his head.*)

I'm sorry, your Grace…my nerves are shot…all this carnage… I can't take anymore. Why don't I just pitch myself over the side and be done with it?

THE DUKE   (*Restrains him.*)

No, no, old friend. I need you now, more than ever… If you continue to feel this way on our return to Lisbon – and you want to kill yourself then – I promise not to stand in your way.

DON PEDRO   That's most generous, your Grace.

THE DUKE   Not at all.

(*The rocket sound intensifies. Everyone falls on deck… And then it dies down… And they rise.*)

DON PEDRO   (*Peering out.*)

I don't believe that's a Giambelli, your Grace. It appears to be an old hulk gotten up to *look* like a Giambelli.

THE DUKE   I knew she'd never pay him his usual fee.

ANTONIA   Whoever designed it did a wonderful job.

THE DUKE   Saved a fortune, too.

DON PEDRO   Doesn't seem to have hit anything, sir.

THE DUKE   It didn't have to. At least a hundred of our ships have broken anchor and scattered to the winds.

ANTONIA   Imagine! A cheap trick.

DON PEDRO   It achieved something all of Drake's galleons couldn't
                    do.

THE DUKE   We should have brought over an imitation Armada –
                    and saved all that money.

ANNOUNCER (O.S.)   On deck…St. Bonaventure.

DIEGO   (*Peering at result of hell-ship attack.*)

                   They're sitting ducks, Sir Francis. Even their galley slaves are exhausted. They're making short, indecisive strokes.

DRAKE   It may be a trap. First they row along sluggishly – then, when they've lulled you to sleep, they pick up the pace and begin rowing briskly. They tried the same thing at Cartagena.

DIEGO   So much happened at Cartagena.

DRAKE   If you were a Cartagena, there was no need to be anywhere else.

DIEGO   I could kick myself for missing it.

DRAKE   You should… Have we isolated the Duke?

DIEGO   It appears that way, Sir Francis.

DRAKE   Good. I'd like to finish him off once and for all…so that the next time he thinks Armada, he'll think again. Let's begin with a drum roll. The dark-complexioned races are terrified of drum-rolls.

                   (*Responds to a look from* DIEGO.)

                   Some of the dark-complexioned races. Follow with a riffle of trumpets. Then strike the topsails, aim the bowguns, and luff up to unleash your broadsides. After that, you can double back leeward so that we're out of range.

DIEGO   How's that again, sir?

DRAKE   Oh, never mind. Just move in a bit.

ANNOUNCER (O.S.)	Deck of the San Martin.
	(*Sound of cannonfire...*THE DUKE, ANTONIA, DON PEDRO *a bit disheveled...perhaps one broken mast to indicate the ship has been mauled.*)
DON PEDRO	They're closing in on us, your Grace.
THE DUKE	Are we prepared?
DON PEDRO	Somewhat...
THE DUKE	(*In disbelief.*)
	What?
	(*Sound of a drum roll.*)
THE DUKE	And what's that sound?
DON PEDRO	A drum roll. As members of a dark-complexioned race, we're supposed to be scared out of our wits.
THE DUKE	That's ridiculous. I *love* drum rolls.
	(*A riffle of trumpets.*)
THE DUKE	*That's* the one that frightens me.
	(*More cannonfire.*)
DON PEDRO	They outnumber us ten to one. Yet they prefer to stand out of range and pound us into garlic.
THE DUKE	Do you know what I'd give for a fresh clove of garlic right now?
ANTONIA	Don't feed their prejudices. The English think you do nothing but sit around and eat garlic all day. Otherwise, I'm sure they'd be delighted to have you invade them.
DON PEDRO	(*Concerned.*)

Our anchors are dragging in loose sand, sir.

THE DUKE   Isn't there any firm sand around here?

DON PEDRO   (*More concerned.*)

The plumb lines say six fathoms. I suggest we retire to Nieuport.

THE DUKE   I don't think so. We've come this far. Might as well stand and fight. That's my feeling for the moment. You might want to check with me a bit later.

(*To* SEAMAN.)

You're in my spot again.

SEAMAN   (*Steps aside.*)

Forgive me, your Grace.

THE DUKE   (*Taking his place.*)

Scurvy coming along?

SEAMAN   Yes, sire. It's the furunculosis I'm worried about.

THE DUKE   What on earth is that?

SEAMAN   Awful. Makes you wish you had scurvy.

THE DUKE   Well…try to get some rest.

SEAMAN   (*Exiting.*)

Rest? That's the worst way to treat furunculosis.

THE DUKE   Then run around the deck. But do go away.

(*Looks out at the water.*)

Amazing. I've finally overcome my seasickness.

ANTONIA	Now you know the cure. Arrange for 140 of Drake's ships to bear down upon you and voila!
DON PEDRO	The lines are closing, sir. They're a pistol shot away.
THE DUKE	(*To* ANTONIA, *as he prepares for battle.*)
	I might just have a proper finale for that chronicle of yours.
ANTONIA	There's no need to get killed in the process.
THE DUKE	I'm not afraid of death. Now that you've convinced me there's an afterlife.
ANTONIA	I can't *guarantee* that it exists.
THE DUKE	Will you *please* make up your mind about that.
DON PEDRO	Our sails and rigging are going, your Grace. Our guns have been blown off deck and there's blood running out of the scuppers.
THE DUKE	Whose blood is it?
DON PEDRO	Some of theirs, some of ours...but they've actually penetrated our hull...we're totally isolated and Drake's entire fleet is intact.
THE DUKE	(*Thoughtfully.*)
	Not a terribly attractive position, is it?
DON PEDRO	(*With gravity.*)
	We're alone, sir. We're beaten. There's a good case for running up the flag.
THE DUKE	No Guzman has ever run up the flag.
ANTONIA	Guzman?

THE DUKE	It's another of our family names. We only use it when we're contemplating surrender. What if we just ran it up halfway?
DON PEDRO	It would be misleading.
THE DUKE	We can't do that... (*Reflects.*) ...and so it ends...
DON PEDRO	I'm afraid so, sir.
THE DUKE	Take an Armada half way around the world – with the best of intentions – and this is your reward...
ANTONIA	(*Looking out to sea.*) I'm sorry to interrupt your lamentations, but isn't that Don Recalde on the *San Juan*?
THE DUKE	(*Peering out.*) I believe you're right. There's de Leyva on the *Rata Encoronada*.
DON PEDRO	And Oquendo on the *Santa Ana*.
ANTONIA	De Bertendona on the Ragazona.
THE DUKE	The *Nepolitana*...
DON PEDRO	The *Gerona*.
ANTONIA	The *Zuniga*.
THE DUKE	The very best we brought from Lisbon. (*Shouts.*) FROM THAT BLOODY CRESCENT!

(*The stage fills again with the tattered yet brilliant flags of the Armada, slowly and beginning to form a crescent. Appropriate music.*)

(*Thrilling music of Spain.*)

THE DUKE   (*As the crescent forms.*)

I certainly hope they remember how to do it.

DON PEDRO   They will, your Grace. It's been drummed into them.

(*The crescent is formed.*)

There you are. What did I tell you!

ANNOUNCER (O.S.)   The deck of Drake's St. Bonaventure

DIEGO   (*Watching the spectacle.*)

Unbelievable! It's like seeing a dragon that's been cut into a hundred pieces become whole again.

DRAKE   If the wind shifts in their favour, England will be every bit as exposed as before. And just our luck, we're out of powder.

DIEGO   Surely you have a surprise up your sleeve.

DRAKE   As a matter of fact, I don't. Why does everyone expect me to come up with surprises?

DIEGO   We could follow them to the Firth of Fourth and hope the North Sea finishes the job for us.

DRAKE   The Firth of Fourth? I can't even pronounce it. Prepare to board them. The Queen will shit if she hears we let them get away.

DIEGO   (*Recoils at the thought.*)

Surely, there's another way to phrase that, your Grace.

DRAKE   As if you hadn't heard worse in your...

(*Sneering.*)

...Bastimentos...

ANNOUNCER (O.S.)   The Duke's *Cabin.*

(*Sound of torrential storm, waters...*THE DUKE *and* ANTONIA *looking half-soaked.*)

THE DUKE   If this keeps us, we'll wash up on the coast of Ireland.

ANTONIA   Good. The Irish adore us. I have close friends in 'The Pale.'

THE DUKE   We may need them.

(DON PEDRO *enters.*)

DON PEDRO   There's chaos above, sir. A party boat from Lisbon has pulled alongside. The deck is awash with courtesans and the galley slaves are aroused and out of control.

ANTONIA   One can hardly blame the poor dears.

DON PEDRO   One of the courtesans insists on seeing you personally.

THE DUKE   (*Muses.*)

I wonder if I know the little baggage...

(*Explains to* ANTONIA.)

I own a small share in the *Inn of the Six Virgins.*

DONA MARIA   (*Bursting in.*)

Know her? You *married* her, you faithless swine.

THE DUKE   Dona Maria! What are you doing here?

(*Introduces her to* ANTONIA.)

My estranged wife.

ANTONIA   It's an enormous pleasure.

DONA MARIA	It is not.
	(*To* DUKE.)
	You didn't expect me to fritter away my life in that stupid orange grove, did you?
	(*Hands him documents.*)
	I need your signature on these tax forms.
THE DUKE	I don't have time for that.
DONA MARIA	Very well, if you'd prefer to lose your villa.
THE DUKE	Oh, all right...
	(*Takes quilled pen.*)
	(DONA MARIA *looks at* ANTONIA – *as* THE DUKE *signs papers.*)
DONA MARIA	(*Re:* ANTONIA.)
	She's so plain...and not the least bit amusing.
ANTONIA	(*Impressed.*)
	Is that your conclusion? On such short notice?
THE DUKE	(*To* ANTONIA.)
	My apologies. She gets a bit cranky at this hour.
DONA MARIA	You poltroon!
THE DUKE	Poltroon, eh? No more party boats for you. It's back to Lisbon you go. There are no nursery facilities available...and the thought of finding you a nanny...
DONA MARIA	I don't want a nanny. I want a husband.

(*Her tone softens.*)

May I suggest, my dear Medina, that you're not the only one who's gone to sea. I, too, have taken a voyage, from the frail and protected shores of childhood to the perilous but ultimately serene harbour of womanhood.

ANTONIA   That's lovely. Did you work on it?

DONA MARIA   Dashed it off.

(*Continues.*)

If I've been remiss in my wifely duties, surely I have years enough to remedy this…

THE DUKE   It's no use, Dona Maria. We've had some pleasant moments, but you must admit, there was something not quite right about our marriage from the start.

DONA MARIA   Such as?

THE DUKE   We've always had different interests. You have your toys, your hopscotch…

DONA MARIA   I nursed you back to financial health.

THE DUKE   I'm aware of that – and I was hoping you could stay on as my bookkeeper.

DONA MARIA   You are *so* mean.

THE DUKE   You're a lovely creature, and I realize this is a bumpy moment for you – but by the time you're twelve, you'll look back and see this as a good development.

DONA MARIA   No, I won't. And it's a lucky thing I registered the orange groves in my name.

THE DUKE   (*Shocked.*)

Dona Maria!

(DRAKE *and* DIEGO *appear, armed to the teeth.*)

THE DUKE   (*Startled.*)

El Draque!

(DRAKE *bows.*)

THE DUKE   Welcome to the San Martin.

(*Introduces group.*)

My estranged wife, Dona Maria...Don Pedro...and Dona Antonia Navarre...

DRAKE   We know each other.

(*To* ANTONIA.)

Why did you leave me?

ANTONIA   You know perfectly well why...

DRAKE   Because I exaggerated a bit on my record trip through the Straits of Magellan? Everyone does that. Magellan did it.

ANTONIA   Magellan most certainly did not. I *knew* Magellan.

THE DUKE   You knew Magellan?

ANTONIA   Slightly. Paracelsus introduced us...at a convention of alchemists.

THE DUKE   (*Increasingly impressed.*)

You knew Paracelsus, too? Could he change base metal into gold?

ANTONIA   Without question. But he wanted to change me, too. He
                    was most irritating. Wanted to change everything.

DRAKE   (*To* ANTONIA.)

                    I liked you. I still do.

ANTONIA   That's enormously flattering, but I'm afraid I've made
                    other plans.

DONA MARIA   She's stolen my husband.

THE DUKE   There was no theft involved.

DRAKE   (*To* ANTONIA.)

                    I thought you liked me…at Santa Fe de Bogota.

ANTONIA   No, it was a Santa Fe de Elena that I liked you. I detested
                    you at Santa Fe de Bogota.

DRAKE   (*Half to himself.*)

                    I must have gotten it all wrong.

THE DUKE   (*Impatient.*)

                    Now look here, Sir Francis. I have a shaky Armada to
                    attend to. I must ask you to state your intentions.

                    (DRAKE *and* DIEGO *draw their swords.*)

DRAKE   The gold…or the woman…

DONA MARIA   Which woman?

THE DUKE   Will you please grow up.

DONA MARIA   I *have* grown up.

THE DUKE   (*To* DRAKE.)

The gold belongs to the King. And as for Dona...

(*Fumbles.*)

ANTONIA   (*Sweetly helping him.*)

Antonia...

THE DUKE   Thank you...Dona Antonia and I have developed
something of a friendship.

ANTONIA   Be still my heart.

THE DUKE   We're lovers.

(DONA MARIA *lets out a loud wail.*)

(ANTONIA *takes her aside to comfort her.*)

THE DUKE   (*To* DRAKE.)

So I'm afraid I can't satisfy either of your demands...
you're welcome to some taffeta.

DRAKE   Don't say taffeta... We're going to have to fight.

ANTONIA   That's absurd. I won't have you fighting over me. I'd
rather go off with Diego.

DONA MARIA   I don't blame you.

DIEGO   (*Seductively, to* ANTONIA.)

I could show you the Bastimentos...

THE DUKE   (*To* DRAKE.)

May I offer you a grappling hook?

DRAKE   I don't grapple.

THE DUKE   (*Helpfully.*)

A pike?

DRAKE   Too unwieldy.

THE DUKE   Then let it be *Juego de Canes...*

DRAKE   (*Puzzled.*)

             Sir?

THE DUKE   It's a form of combat in which the opponents circle
             round on miniature bulls and fling canes at one another.

DRAKE   (*Considers.*)

             I *am* an excellent horseman.

DIEGO   (*Cautions.*)

             Bulls are another matter, your Excellency.

DRAKE   I don't see why. You have bulls aboard?

THE DUKE   We can improvise.

DRAKE   I'll need to be upwind.

THE DUKE   Granted.

             (*Calls out.*)

             Don Pedro!

             (DON PEDRO *opens cabin door. Two galley slaves
             appear – on hands and knees – bulls' horns affixed to
             their heads...*   DRAKE *and* THE DUKE *mount
             their 'bulls.'.*)

THE DUKE   (*Raises a cane.*)

             All right, El Draque, let's see what you're made of...

DRAKE   With pleasure, Captain *Garlic.*

DON PEDRO   (*To* DIEGO.)

                         Care for a clove?

DIEGO   How very kind.

                         (*He takes one.*)

                         (DRAKE *and* THE DUKE *begin to fight – as the storm grows more intense.*)

DONA MARIA   (*Looking on – to* ANTONIA.)

                         You're wasting your time. He'll never stay with you. We do this all the time...find others lovers...and then we always get back together...

ANTONIA   It sounds exhausting. Why bother?

DONA MARIA   We do it to spice up the marriage.

ANTONIA   (*Impressed, again.*)

                         You're remarkably precocious, aren't you?

                         (*Sound of the storm intensifying.*)

DON PEDRO   (*Comes between combatants.*)

                         We'll have to resume this at another time, your Grace. We've taken on a frightful amount of water, and the ship has been torn asunder.

THE DUKE   (*Drawing back.*)

                         There will be another chapter, El Draque.

DRAKE   I look forward to it.

(*As lights darken...shouts, screams...deafening sound of waves, as if cabin is being engulfed.*)

DRAKE (*V.O.*)   I'm taking some taffeta.

GERMAN WOMAN
(O.S.)   Meine Gute...Meinse gute... Fragen Sie doch...Meine Gute...

ANNOUNCER (O.S.)   Days later... A strip of beach...

(THE DWARF *staggers on stage, soaked, befuddled.*)

(SOUND *of Irish music...* HE *knows where he is, brightens, does an Irish dance.*)

ANNOUNCER (O.S.)   Another strip of beach...

> (THE DUKE, ANTONIA, DON PEDRO *lie there, exhausted – in loincloths...having just washed ashore.*)

ANTONIA   Freezing in those waters. Any idea of where we are?

DON PEDRO   Either Ireland, Scotland or Denmark.

ANTONIA   (*Shivering.*)

So long as there's a warm bath.

THE DUKE   The King's not going to be happy about losing that Armada. He expected a great deal more for his money.

ANTONIA   I thought it performed admirably, under the circumstances. He'll see that when he reads my chronicle.

(*Looks around.*)

Where *is* my chronicle? I can't believe I went through that entire voyage for nothing.

THE DUKE   I'm offended.

ANTONIA   (*Puts her arm around him.*)

Don't be foolish. But I would like it back.

(*As* SHE *looks around,* MCCABB *appears.*)

THE DUKE   Oh, good, a friendly face.

MCCABB   Stop and identify yourselves.

THE DUKE   With pleasure...the Duke of Medina, Don Pedro Ferrara

(*Looks at* ANTONIA *and starts groping.*)

ANTONIA	(*Helping him again.*)
	Antonia Navarre…
	(*To* DUKE.)
	I can't believe you…
THE DUKE	I've never been good at names.
	(*To* SAVAGE.)
	Enormous pleasure to meet you.
MCCABB	McLaghlin McCabb.
ANTONIA	We're in luck. It's Ireland…
MCCABB	(*Continuing.*)
	…Thane of the Darty Mountains…
THE DUKE	I've heard so much about them. Lovely in autumn.
MCCABB	…with the blood of a hundred Spanish pigs on my hands…
	(*Two similar savage-types appear, with raised galleaxes.*)
THE DUKE	(*As his party is being led off.*)
	This is a mistake. They think we're French or something. It will all be straightened out in no time.
	(*To captors.*)
	We've given your people *so* much help…

ANNOUNCER (O.S.)   Strip of beach... a bit later...

(DWARF *still dancing...* OLD MAN *appears.*)

DWARF   (*Stops dancing.*)

Oh, good. A friend...

OLD MAN   I'm not a friend. I'm a leprechaun.

DWARF   Leprechauns aren't real.

OLD MAN   That's what they say...

DWARF   (*Catches on.*)

You're a leprechaun impersonator...

OLD MAN   How did you know?

DWARF   I'm a dwarf impersonator.

OLD MAN   Could have fooled me.

DWARF   (*Pleased.*)

Nice to have some company.

(HE *extends his arm.* OLD MAN *takes it. Music starts up. They go dancing O.S. together.*)

ANNOUNCER (O.S.)   Meanwhile…

(*That nearby strip of beach. A stake* (*broken mast.*). THE DUKE, ANTONIA, DON PEDRO *chained to it. Some time has passed.*)

DON PEDRO   Did you get some sleep, your Grace?

THE DUKE   Very little.

(*Looks at* ANTONIA, *who is barely covered by her loincloth.*)

Someone kept tossing about and snuffling.

ANTONIA   I've never slept tied to a stake before.

THE DUKE   One tries to keep one's head elevated.

ANTONIA   One will remember that when it's time for one's nap.

THE DUKE   Just our luck – to be captured by the one man in Ireland who hates Spaniards.

DON PEDRO   Perhaps he was abused by one as a child.

ANTONIA   He's from a wild clan. I know their methods. They'll do anything – as long as it's wild.

DON PEDRO   It's a wonder he hasn't chopped off our heads. He has a stack of them outside his hut – for decorative purposes. All from the Armada.

THE DUKE   Anyone we know?

DON PEDRO   We know all of them.

THE DUKE   Just keep pretending we have lots of doubloons.

ANTONIA   (*Looks at her loincloth.*)

Where? Where do we keep them?

THE DUKE   (*As* MCCABB *and two clansmen approach.*)

Here he comes. From the look on his face, we'll never see Lisbon again.

ANTONIA   He always has that look. Haven't you noticed? It's his one look.

MCCABB   One of your commanders has agreed to pay your ransom. A barge stands ready for your return to Spain.

(*Clansmen untie* DON PEDRO *and* THE DUKE.)

THE DUKE   But what about...?

(*Fumbles.*)

ANTONIA   (*Glares at him.*)

Antonia...Antonia Navarre.

THE DUKE   That will never happen again.

MCCABB   There's been no mention of the wench...off with you.

(*Two clansmen lead away* DON PEDRO *and* THE DUKE.)

THE DUKE   (*Struggling.*)

But we can't just leave her.

DON PEDRO   You'll soon forget her, your Grace...

THE DUKE   I know...but I've gotten used to her...

DON PEDRO   She's just a writer...

THE DUKE   I realize that...but I rather like her work...

(*Suddenly strains forward – shouts.*)

I LOVE HER...

ANNOUNCER (O.S.)   Yet another strip of beach…nearby.

(DRAKE *staggers onstage…wet, disheveled…followed by* DONA MARIA…*in the same state.*)

DRAKE   I recognize you. You're married to THE Duke.

DONA MARIA   If you call that married…

DRAKE   Could you like someone like me?

DONA MARIA   Of course. You're rich and famous.

DRAKE   I suppose I am famous…but I'm not as rich as they say. Most of my money is buried.

DONA MARIA   But you know where it is.

DRAKE   Of course.

DONA MARIA   Where is it?

DRAKE   It's in a crab furrow in the Bastimentos.

DONA MARIA   Oh.

(*Thinks, then turns.*)

Could you dry my back. You can use sand if you like.

(SHE *sits.* HE *sits beside her, begins to dry her.*)

DONA MARIA   (*Flirtatiously.*)

And watch those hands, El Draque.

(DRAKE *colours, continues, cautiously, to dry her.*)

ANNOUNCER (O.S.)   One month later...Spain...The Escorial...The Throne Room of Phillip the Second...

(THE KING *is on his knees, in his customary position, affixing his seal to documents. An* AIDE *enters.*)

AIDE   Your Grace. The heroes of the Armada are here.

PHILLIP   How exciting. Bring them to me at once.

(*Celebratory music...a burst of flowers and confetti...as the puzzled* DUKE *and* DON PEDRO *enter the throne room.*)

PHILLIP   Congratulations, dear sirs... Approach the throne and receive the thanks of a grateful Empire.

(*Still confused,* THEY *kneel as* PHILLIP *puts diamond pendants about their necks.*)

THE DUKE   This is very kind, your Grace. But may I ask why we're being congratulated?

PHILLIP   Don't be coy, Medina.

(*Unfurls document.*)

It's right here in this dispatch.

(*Reads.*)

"Drake has had his leg shot off and England is ours..."

THE DUKE   But that's impossible. Parma never came out for the invasion and the Armada broke down in the North Sea.

DON PEDRO   I can verify that, your Grace. No more than thirty of our ships escaped.

PHILLIP   That's odd. This spy of ours is generally reliable.

(*To* AIDE.)

Bring him to me.

(AIDE *exits.*)

PHILLIP

Chap named Giambelli. Used to design hell-ships for the English. Paid him a fortune to come over to our side...

(AIDE *comes in with* GIAMBELLI, *who wears a jewel-encrusted uniform.*)

PHILLIP

Well...what about this?

(*Outburst of invective in Italian from* GIAMBELLI.)

AIDE

(*Translating.*)

He says he may have been wrong about the invasion, but he'll stake his reputation on Drake's leg being shot off...

PHILLIP

What a nuisance...Take him away.

(AIDE *leads off* GIAMBELLI, *still shouting outraged imprecations.*)

PHILLIP

(*Muttering.*)

The little garlic ball... Well, this does change things a bit, Medina. I had a holiday named in your honor.

THE DUKE

I'm sorry if I've disappointed you. And I'm sure your subjects will ignore the holiday.

PHILLIP

Part of the fleet returned, I suppose it could have been worse.

THE DUKE

Since your Grace isn't too displeased, I wonder if I might ask a favour. There is a woman who lies rotting

	as a prisoner in the Darty Mountains. It would mean a great deal to me if you paid her ransom.
PHILLIP	I'm surprised at you, Medina. Some little baggage. Out of the question. Besides, I'll need every penny for the next Armada. You wouldn't by any chance be interested?
THE DUKE	No, your Grace. One Armada is quite sufficient.
PHILLIP	Well, if you change your mind…what *are* your plans?
THE DUKE	Return to Andalusia, I suppose, and try to revive my groves.
PHILLIP	Good luck to you, Medina. And thank you for helping out.
THE DUKE	Not at all, your Grace.
	(*Turns to go – then lashes out.*)
	And she's *not* baggage.
PHILLIP	(*Unused to impertinence.*)
	Are you serious?!
THE DUKE	Forgive me. I'm new at romance.
	(H E *storms off,* D O N P E D R O *at his side.*)
	(*Outside* PHILLIP'S *chambers.*)
DON PEDRO	I'm sorry about Antonia.
THE DUKE	What does Phillip know about love! Spends the whole day in that draughty castle – on his knees, no less.
DON PEDRO	I wondered about that. Is it religious devotion?

THE DUKE	No, he gave that up long ago. He got down on his knees one day, found it comfortable and never got up again.
DON PEDRO	I thought perhaps your Grace might require some help with his groves?
THE DUKE	I appreciate the thought. But my plans are to sit and stare hopelessly at the horizon. Goodbye, dear friend.
DON PEDRO	Goodbye, your Grace.
THE DUKE	I'm not quite sure what we accomplished, but I could never have pulled it off without you.
DON PEDRO	It was quite an Armada, wasn't it?
THE DUKE	One of the best, while it lasted.

(THEY *embrace.*)

(Lights down, lights up.)

ANNOUNCER (O.S.)   Andalusia...THE DUKE'S Villa

(HE *sits, in near darkness, vacantly staring ahead.*)

(*A servant enters, with a tray.*)

SERVANT   Some orange juice, your Grace.

THE DUKE   No, thank you.

SERVANT   It's from your favorite grove.

THE DUKE   I don't care. I've given it up.

SERVANT   What *is* your pleasure?

THE DUKE   I don't have any. I just want to sit here – and not have any pleasure.

SERVANT   May I light another candle?

THE DUKE   No, I prefer it the way it is – depressing.

(*Looks up.*)

You're new here, aren't you?

SERVANT   Arrived here only this morning.

THE DUKE   Well, see to it that I'm not too comfortable.

SERVANT   As you wish, sir.

THE DUKE   What *is* it about you?

SERVANT   (*Turns.*)

I have no idea, your Grace.

(*Spills tray – with juice – in* DUKE'S *lap.*)

THE DUKE   (*Leaping up.*)

Oh, for God's sakes. I should have known.

(*It registers.*)

Of course.

(HE *tears off servant's head-dress, confident it's* ANTONIA. *It's* SIR FRANCIS DRAKE.)

THE DUKE   El Draque! In my own villa! Hold on while I fetch my Arquebus.

(*As* HE *roots around,* SERVANT *removes mask. It is* ANTONIA.)

THE DUKE   It's you. I knew it all along.

ANTONIA   You did not.

THE DUKE   What if my heart had stopped beating?

ANTONIA   There was only the slimmest chance that would happen.

THE DUKE   Yet you took that chance.

ANTONIA   You needed some shaking up.

THE DUKE   How did you get away?

ANTONIA   I bribed McLaghlin with my body.

THE DUKE   You didn't.

ANTONIA   I tried…but he doesn't lean that way.

THE DUKE   I *knew* there was something about him.

ANTONIA   Actually, I told him the story of my life. He gave me some doubloons and made me promise never to come back again. How can you sit here in this dark room?

(SHE *lights a candle.*)

THE DUKE	My hair turned white during the Voyage. Frankly, I'm a little embarrassed about it.
ANTONIA	You shouldn't be. It was white when we first met.
THE DUKE	It's whiter now.
ANTONIA	Distinguished.
THE DUKE	White.
ANTONIA	I love you.
THE DUKE	I love you, too.
ANTONIA	I've finished my chronicle. Would you like to hear it?
THE DUKE	Not just now.
ANTONIA	I'll read it anyway.

(*Produces folio.*)

"Don Pedro delivered the wonderful news. At long last, the Armada was completed. "Oh, Good," said the King. "Who can we get to lead it?"

THE DUKE   (*Answers question.*)

"The Governor of Castile. Excellent chap and he loves Armadas."

HE *takes folio, sets it aside, sweeps her up in his arms.*

| ANTONIA | I haven't come to the good part. |
| THE DUKE | (*Wickedly.*) |

Neither have I.

| ANTONIA | I worked *so* hard on it. |

THE DUKE   It was worth every second.

ANTONIA   (*Tenderly.*)

                  Alonzo…

THE DUKE   Antonia.

ANTONIA   You remembered.

                  (HE *carries her off.*)

                      (*Pennants, music.*)

                          CURTAIN

THE TRIAL

CHARACTER LIST

JONES   A middle-aged, casually dressed tourist, reunit-
                       ing with a college acquaintance.

WAINRIGHT   A middle-aged man dressed in a smoking jacket
                       and slippers.

(*Set in contemporary London.* JONES *and* WAIN-RIGHT, *sit facing each other in the comfortably appointed parlour room of a townhouse. The home belongs to* WAINRIGHT.)

WAINRIGHT (*To* JONES, *who has just arrived.*)

Awfully nice to see you, Jones. May I offer you a brandy?

JONES That would be nice.

(WAINRIGHT *walks to bar/cabinet, pours two brandies.*)

WAINRIGHT (*As he returns with drinks.*)

Cigar?

JONES I don't believe so.

(WAINRIGHT *takes cigar out of humidor.*)

WAINRIGHT Little Dominican. They've done wonders with the soil. Surpassed Havana, if you ask me.

JONES (*Shrugs.*)

Why not?

(HE *takes cigar,* WAINRIGHT *lights it for him.* THEY *sip brandy, smoke….*)

WAINRIGHT Well, then, what brings you to London?

JONES   Vacation. My wife and I thought we'd treat our eleven-year-old daughter to the Grand Tour. They're off exploring the countryside. I heard you were living here and thought I'd call and ask if I could drop by. You *do* remember me?

WAINRIGHT   Oh, yes, skinny chap from the East, always chewing on your lip. You've gained some weight.

JONES   Nice of you to point that out.

WAINRIGHT   I haven't exactly remained slim as a reed.

(*Pats middle.*)

It's that area here.

JONES   I know it well.

WAINRIGHT   How did you find out I was in London?

JONES   I attended a reunion in Kansas City. Thirtieth, to be exact.

WAINRIGHT   You'd never been back?

JONES   No. Some years ago, I was up for a professorship at Brown and called our old school for a copy of my transcript and diploma. They said they had no record of my ever having studied there.

WAINRIGHT   As if you'd dreamed the whole thing.

JONES   So they implied. The Brown people began to think I'd falsified my credentials. I did find my records eventually...in the attic...all yellowed over...but I suppose I've never forgiven our alma mater.

WAINRIGHT   ...Until the reunion...

JONES	Tick, Tick, tick...we're getting on now. Who knows how many more we'll have.
WAINRIGHT	(*Pleasantly.*)
	How was it?
JONES	The reunion? Quite moving, actually. They had all gone into the shoe business...*thrived* in the shoe business.
WAINRIGHT	I recall they would spend a great deal of time shining their shoes. Are they still at it?
JONES	Shining away. You see all those shoes and the effect is blinding. But our friends have held up well. I had expected to be amused by the experience, but not moved. Fraternities aren't taken seriously these days, but there *was* a bond.
WAINRIGHT	So I'm told.
JONES	I hardly expected you to show up, but I did wonder what had become of you. A fellow named Chip said you had moved to London.
WAINRIGHT	I remember Chip. How is Chip? Chip still fidgety?
JONES	More so than ever.
WAINRIGHT	Lost his thumb in a bread slicer, as I recall.
JONES	Make anyone fidgety.
WAINRIGHT	I should think so.
	(*Takes a sip of brandy.*)
	So here we are.
JONES	Here we are.

WAINRIGHT	I suppose you've come to ask about the trial.
JONES	It *was* a trial, wasn't it?
WAINRIGHT	Of a kind. Plenty of judges, but unfortunately, no defence attorney.
JONES	I recall being in the dormitory and someone calling out: "We've caught the thief." We all went rushing into the Chapter Room.
WAINRIGHT	And there I was – with my hand in the cookie jar.
JONES	I suppose this is painful.
WAINRIGHT	It was then.
JONES	Then let me continue. There had been some thievery. The Seniors decided to set a trap – a wallet bulging with money, which they set out on a table…like cheese for a mouse. They all hid inside a locker and waited. You came out, looked at the wallet….
WAINRIGHT	…and picked it up. I *do* remember, you know.
JONES	(*Caught up in the story, doesn't hear this.*)
	They pounced on you, hustled you off to the basement, and we all listened as they read the charges. You sat there, your eyes were wide, your mouth open, like a great fish, with a hook in its jaw. If I'm not mistaken, you were wearing a cream-coloured suit.
	(*Opens mouth wide, demonstrates.*)
WAINRIGHT	It's entirely possible. I've always favoured cream. But why do you present this to me now? After thirty years?
JONES	Curiosity. Intense curiosity. I've never stopped thinking about it…wondering about the effect on your life…

your schooling…your work…your sex life, for that matter…

WAINRIGHT   I can assure you it's had no effect on my sex life. Might very well have kicked it up a bit. For a decade or so, sex was my sole preoccupation…affairs, mistresses, shady ladies…anything in a skirt that came my way… An Arab boy, too, if you must know.

(*Reflects.*)

I do miss those days. But of course I think about our trial. How could I not? Was the episode central to my existence? Hardly. I stayed on for the semester, you'll remember.

JONES   I didn't realize that. I must have blocked it out.

WAINRIGHT   I suppose I needed to demonstrate how brave I was. No one spoke to me, looked at me. Half-assed Coventry is what it was. I found it all amusing and actually felt sorry for the poor bastards…judging me… I'm sure they were more uncomfortable than I was…

JONES   I must have been one of the poor bastards.

WAINRIGHT   So you must. All of you.

(*Pauses, recalls.*)

JONES   And then you left.

WAINRIGHT   Went off to Oxford…my parents had some money… Got a proper education…married, divorced…took that long time off for promiscuity…then married again…

(HE *takes framed photograph of his second wife from mantelpiece, shows it to* JONES.)

JONES   (*Staring at photograph.*)

                    Lovely. Has that underbite, that British underbite I've
                    always found appealing.

WAINRIGHT   That's two of us…It's been a happy marriage, can't
                    imagine a better one. Along the way, I accumulated a
                    fortune as a commodities broker. In the overall, the trial
                    "episode" might have been a good thing. Got me out of
                    that college cowtown, for one thing. Of course, I think
                    about the episode now and then…the humiliation…I
                    did feel humiliated. But you see, the day I took the
                    money, *considered* taking it – I never really took it –
                    was the first time I'd ever done such a thing. There had
                    been money missing before, some of mine, actually…
                    so I knew there was another thief in the house. And I
                    suppose I knew that eventually I'd receive a visit of this
                    kind.

JONES   You *knew*?

WAINRIGHT   Oh, yes, I was convinced of it – assuming I lived long
                    enough. Now I've told you how the episode has affected
                    my life. My question to you, dear fellow is – how has it
                    affected yours?

                    (WAINRIGHT *sits back, takes a satisfied sip of his
                    brandy, awaits* JONES' *reaction. The two men stare
                    at each other.* JONES, *ever so slightly, shifts his weight
                    uncomfortably. They continue to stare at each other.*)

                    FREEZE

                    (*And black.*)

REVIEWS

Julius Novick, New York Times, July 12, 1970
"Is This Any Way to Run a Steambath?" – Review of Steambath

Although He is widely alleged to be dead, God still receives a considerable amount of attention from modern writers. After all, if you want to make metaphors for the absurdity and nastiness of the world we live in, one way to do it is to imagine the sort of absurd and nasty person (modern gods are highly anthropomorphic) who would create and maintain such a world. If you are bitter and angry at the world (which often goes with a perception of it as absurd and nasty), you can relieve your feelings by demeaning and deriding the God you have created. And if your bent is toward comedy, you can have a sardonic and blasphemous good time in playing on the incongruity-gap between the conventional image of God and your own disreputable version of Him.

Thus, in Joseph Heller's "Catch-22," Yossarian expostulates to Lieutenant Scheisskopf's wife: "Good God, how much reverence can you have for a Supreme Being who finds it necessary to include such phenomena as phlegm and tooth decay in His divine system of creation? When you consider the opportunity and power He had to really do a job, and then look at the stupid, ugly, little mess He made of it instead, His sheer incompetence is almost staggering."

And thus Bruce Jay Friedman's new play "Steambath," in which God is a Puerto Rican steambath attendant named Morty.

Unlike Heller's God, however, Friedman's God is not a bungler; He just doesn't give a damn. As He tidies up the steambath, he casually addresses orders over his shoulder to a TV monitor of some sort: "Give that girl on the bus a run in her body stocking, and close that branch of Schrafft's." Orders for deaths and mutilations are equally casual. As for prayers, pleas, remonstrances, and complaints, Morty is simply not interested. "You say another word, baby, I'll become wrathful and vengeance-seeking. All right, everybody, campfire time."

Morty's steambath is where people go when they're dead, to tell their stories for his amusement. Until Morty is ready for them, they pass their time as best they can. An old wanderer tells stories of his adventures: "I once stood in an Algerian pissoir and watched the head of a good friend of mine come rolling up against my size 12 moccasins like a bowling ball." A slob spits on the floor, eats an orange, cuts his toe-nails, and watches television. A pretty, artless blonde girl trips cheerfully in, takes a shower center-stage, and trips cheerfully away again. (I know what you're wondering. Yes.) A broker checks the Dow-Jones listings, conveniently projected for his benefit on a screen that comes down from the ceiling. A couple of homosexuals do a campy song-and-dance number about the joys of being 65.

Only one man in the steambath refuses to accept his fate, a young man named Tandy who has finally, after a number of lousy years, built himself a life that he likes. He has divorced his unfaithful wife, established a wonderful rapport with his little daughter, made peace with his mother, and found a devoted girl friend; furthermore, a Hollywood studio is interested in the novel he's writing. He has everything to live for, and he demands to be allowed to go back and live. And then, in the best scene in the play, he is forced by Morty's massive indifference to admit that his friend bores him, that he has to take his daughter to puppet shows because he has nothing to say to her, and so on, and that this hard-won, exemplary modern life is empty. His sudden death has not suddenly made it meaningless; it was meaningless all along.

Like all good plays about the after-life, "Steambath" is really about this life; and like all good fantasies, it is really an attempt to convey a set of feelings about reality. If you are left unmoved by the notion that God might be a Puerto Rican steambath attendant, "Steambath" is unlikely to be of much interest to you; but if you are disposed to accept this idea as intriguing and stimulating, as I was, you will probably find that the play contains a good deal of quite distinguished comic writing.

Furthermore, it has been in most respects very well presented. Ivor David Balding has produced it with an admirable determination not to cut corners, and Anthony Perkins, who directed, takes the play seriously without forgetting that it is a comedy. They have realized that the playwright's conceit depends largely on the actuality of that steambath, and have taken great pains with it. David Mitchell's set is admirably solid, and it exhales splendid billows of steam.

The acting is generally good, too. Conrad Bain, as the old wanderer who once slept with the fifth richest woman in Sydney, Australia, has a noble farewell-to-arms speech which he enacts nobly. Annie Rachel, the pretty little blonde who takes the shower, is delicately attractive and sweetly confiding. And Hector Elizondo is really remarkable as God; I doubt I have ever seen indifference played with such effortless strength. Elizondo concentrates on cleaning up his steambath – that's what he really cares about – and seldom seems to be paying much attention to the inmates; but he is always intensely there: this God doesn't mess around.

I must not neglect to mention too the really zonking epiphany that is provided for Morty at the end of Act I, when He shows Himself in all His glory, with music and lights and everything. It is a parody, of course, and a funny one; yet it is a little awesome, too.

But why, I wonder, with all this to be said for it, is "Steambath" never quite as satisfying as it ought to be?

And why, you may ask, have I said nothing about the fact that the central role of Tandy, the rebellious hero of "Steambath," is being played by the director, Anthony Perkins, after having been performed during several fraught weeks of previews by Dick Shawn, Rip Torn, and Charles Grodin? Well, Perkins, within the limits of his boyish personal, is a very good actor – personable, easy-going, comfortable to watch – and he plays some aspects of the character quite nicely. I could believe that Tandy used to teach art appreciation at the Police Academy, and that he was writing a historical novel about Charlemagne. But Perkins is just not mature enough, aggressive enough, nervous enough, hip enough, Jewish enough, perhaps, to play all the complications of the character. After all these years, Perkins remains a Boy Scout.

But the trouble with "Steambath" goes deeper than that. The characters, except for Morty, have not been very specifically imagined. (What kind of hero is named Tandy? Who is he? Where does he come from?) And often the writing is just not sharp enough from moment to moment. Friedman is not just writing about the human condition at large; he seems to be trying to express some perceptions of the life around him, and around us, right here and now – the life that includes Gristede's and Mounds bars and Newsweek and knowing, or not knowing, who Norman Podhoretz is – by giving the familiar a twist into the incongruous and the grotesque. Often he succeeds. But sometimes the incongruities and grotesqueries are not sufficiently rooted in reality, and so appear arbitrary and pointless. And Friedman's obscenities and racial insults, which seemed so liberating in his first play, "Scuba Duba," now sometimes seem just self-indulgent.

Still, "Steambath" is the only show in town in which God says, "You want to discuss the relativity of mass, the Lorentz Transformation, galactic intelligence, I'll give you that, too. Just don't bug Me. Don't be no wise ass." And Friedman is not just a blasphemously funny writer; if you haven't come across a good perception of the Absurd lately, this one is personal and cogent and contemporary.

Harold Clurman, NAT, October 30, 1967
Review of Scuba Duba

At the New Theatre on East 54th Streeth. Bruce Jay Friedman's Scuba Duba is f-u-n-n-y. It is also funny.

I find it difficult to fathom on my own reaction beyond the cachinnation which the initial contact with the play produced in me. My funny bone had been struck a considerable whack but I could not make out the exact nature of the effect beyond its immediate physical manifestation. There is laughter and laughter, and though the theatergoer in need of pastime may be entirely satisfied when his risibilities have been aroused, the critic should not content himself with the mere notation of the fact.

In spelling out the key word above I mean to indicate the unease I experienced as I laughed. There as something sad about the play which Peter Larkin's pretty set, the vulgarity of the language, the blatant jokes, the general extravagance of the proceedings did not efface. My head had been hammered, yet I was left with a hold in my heart.

Stripped of theatrical embellishments (Jacques Levy's production is most apt) the play's plot makes a clear point. Harold Wonder, a young New Yorker on his vacation on the Riviera with his wife and two children, strongly suspects that she has run off with a black scuba diver. Frantic with anxiety, Harold spills his troubles out on Miss Janus, a marvelously stacked American neighbor who comes in to visit him in a bikini. He has no eye for her readily available blandishments though he puts up with her simple-mindedness.

He makes an overseas call to his mother, whose consolation consists

of a combination of vomitous bromides and aggression. He summons his psychoanalyst, who arrives with Cheyenne, a middle-aged floozy of shameless candor. The doctor's ministrations may be summed up as a kind of Zen doubletalk which drives Harold to the verge of violence. Unable to calm Harold, the analyst takes Cheyenne to bed.

Harold's wife, Jean, makes an appearance with her skin diver friend, a clownish black named Foxtrot out of a mental Disneyland accoutered in the devilish paraphernalia of his profession. But Jean is not sleeping with him. Her lover is Reddington, a suave coffee-colored Negro of a very rational demeanor.

Jean tells Harold that he lacks continental delicacy or seductive finesse (she succumbs to his advances only in the bathroom) and that she must leave him. Reddington tries to appease Harold's bewildered fury with the admonition that he ought to accept the situation with civilized poise. At this point Harold goes berserk, strikes the solar plexus of an intruding bore of a tourist, and is ultimately left alone with the children. Though Miss Janus, the receptive lady of appetizing contours invites him to join her in a party at her place, Harold still hankers after his coldly obtuse wife at whom he howls his perennial passion.

In all the simplicity of his soul he doesn't want the dumb siren he can have, only the dumb wife he can't. Pathetic. One surmises that this is not an objective story told for fun but a subjectively painful tale wrestled from the author's hectic experience! But it's nuts, and he tells it in maniacal self-derision.

The play is written and directed in a style that might be set down as that of the old *Esquire* and the new *Playboy* blue joke cartoons, raw in color, jocular in design. There are little side dishes. First there is a French cop who instead of arresting a lunatic "anarchist" who nightly robs Harold's house, bawls Harold out for being an American and thus an impostor. (The cop concludes the scene by leading the foreigners in the *Marseillaise*.) Then there is the house agent who insists that all of her tenants are famous movie stars (she takes Foxtrot for Sidney Poitier) and acts the *femme fatal* with every male she encounters. The show's every detail is kooky.

But it is not any falsity I fear in this shebang, not the stylization but the verisimilitude. This is not satire, it is naturalism! It is also "nihilism." What Friedman, willy-nilly, is telling us from the frazzled depths of his being is that he, they, *we* are all living in a loony bin in which anything goes. And that there's no use feeling anything about it since nothing is what it seems or is given out to be. We are puppets playing balanced games on a freak stage.

When Harold attacks his wife's companions in the insulting lingo of the gutter he is altogether innocent of any racial slur; he is simply reacting to the turmoil of his cracked brain in which nothing is firmly established or substantial. He is a hobgoblin with straw suffering where the organs of intelligence and emotion are supposed to dwell. Only enough of the original human is retained to emit squawks of distress which remind us of the removed parts. When a Russian long ago wrote such a play (on another level, with a different motivation) he ended by having an actor turn to the audience and cry out: "What are you laughing about, this is you!" We guffaw unabashed: we don't care.

Am I taking *Scuba Duba* too seriously? As I indicated at the outset, I too was jostled into mirth by this uproariously declarative farce. It is a thing typical of a contemporary America: spontaneous in forthrightness whereby the author strips himself and us of all phony pretense of decorum or cultivation. I too admired the free-swinging skill of the presentation. But I left the theatre with a slight ache. The play is more depressing in its hilarity than *Who's Afraid of Virginia Woolf?* in its drama, more devastating in its zaniness than Pinter in his constriction. What troubles me is that so few recognize this.

As Harold Wonder, Jerry Orbach excels because his funny stuff is solidly rounded on sincerity which the character must have, and which is at the base of Friedman's inspiration. Brenda Smiley's figure commands our scrupulous attention and she has been admirably directed to give Miss Janus the right touch of amiable nitwittedness. Rita Karin is killingly idiotic as the come hither, hip-swaying French housekeeper. Ken Olfson has the suitably glazed solemnity as the head shrinker who recommends that Harold see life "sideways." And Cleavon Little makes a fantastic and agile sprite of Foxtrot. There are a few forced notes and one somewhat dull spot but everyone plays in pitch.

Since early September I have witnessed a number of stage events which I have failed to report and to some of which I may give fuller attention at a later date. Here in the meantime are fleeting notes.

The Joffrey Ballet, a youthfully pleasing and expert company, delighted me in *Cello Concerto* to Vivaldi's score and intrigued me in the mixed media tribute to *Astarte*.

Judy Garland with some vocal insecurity in the lower register still touches me deeply. She is incapable of making a graceless movement.

Her dramatic instinct is faultless; her every gesture suggests a large area of never wholly realized power. But this lack of completeness is somehow moving, draws us closer to her.

Marlene Dietrich, pearl-visaged, streamlined phoenix, deserves extended commentary. Do not inquire about her voice or delivery. It is the person herself with her staunch wistfulness, her eyes that gaze at us from the hazy corridors of the past, that matters. She is courteous and aloof; there is a gravity about her now that has little to do with the naughty froufrou of the old days. For all the exquisite flamboyance of her dress, the total impression is of an imperviousness to which one gladly gives obeisance.

After the Rain by John Bowen (Golden Theatre) is a play of so-called ideas. It is a bloodless parable about the rise and hallowness of dictatorship. I did not mind its didacticism but I was anasthetized by its banality.

At the Lyceum, Max Adrian offers a one-man show, By *George* (Bernard Shaw). The actor's speech is distinct—the hint of brogue in the accent brings out the element of Irish blarney in the master's prose—and his effort is valiant. The selection of material offers us only a tracing of Shaw's career, but even a little of his language and spirit does much to compensate for Broadway.